CHRISTIAN LIGHT EDUCATION
Reading Series

Happy Hearts

Second Grade Reader
Book 2

Compiled by Ruth K. Hobbs

CHRISTIAN LIGHT
EDUCATION

Harrisonburg, Virginia
(540) 434-0750   www.christianlight.org

CHRISTIAN LIGHT
Reading Series

Grade 1
I Wonder

Grade 2, book 1
Helping Hands

Grade 2, book 2
Happy Hearts

Grade 3
Doors to Discovery

Grade 4
Bridges Beyond

Grade 5
Open Windows

Grade 6
Calls to Courage

Grade 7
The Road Less Traveled

Grade 8
Where Roads Diverge

HAPPY HEARTS
Christian Light Education, a division of
Christian Light Publications
Harrisonburg, VA 22802
©1999 Christian Light Publications, Inc.
All rights reserved.
Printed in China

Ninth Printing, 2022

ISBN: 978-0-87813-935-4

Border: Hemera/Thinkstock

Table *of* Contents

208

v

*"Children, obey your parents in the Lord:
for this is right."* – Ephesians 6:1

The Lost Shoes

Why did Eva Mae ask God to help her at last?

Eva Mae liked to work. And she liked to sing as she worked. That is why Mama called her Sunshine Girl.

But Eva Mae had one bad **habit.** It was all because she liked to go **barefooted.** Even when it was cold outside, she liked to go barefooted in the house. As soon as she got

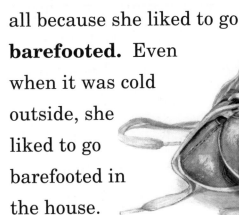

home from school, she kicked off her shoes. Then she went barefooted till bedtime.

To be sure, that was not the bad habit. The bad habit was that when she kicked off her shoes, she did not put them away. When tomorrow came, she did not know where she had left them. And that **certainly** made a lot of trouble.

Mama told Eva Mae over and over, "Sunshine Girl, when you take off your shoes, you must put them in a safe place. You must remember where you put them."

But when Eva Mae was playing, it was too much of a bother to find a safe place for her shoes. She just kicked them off and went on playing.

She forgot how much bother it was to find the shoes when they were lost. She forgot how long it always took to find them. She forgot how much of a **nuisance** it was to dry

3

them when she had left them out in the rain.

At last, Mama said, "You have a bad habit, Sunshine Girl. And you are not trying to do any better. You are not trying to obey me. The next time you must hunt for your shoes, I will have to think of a way to help you remember to obey."

The next Saturday, Eva Mae ran barefooted most of the day. It had rained on Friday. There were the best puddles to splash in.

In the afternoon Daddy was going to the store. "May I please go along?" asked Eva Mae.

"Certainly," said Daddy. "Get your shoes on—no bare feet in the store."

Eva Mae ran upstairs. She ran into all the rooms trying to find her shoes. They were not there.

She ran downstairs.

"Where are my shoes? Did anyone see my shoes?"

"I didn't," said Mama.

"I didn't," said her sisters.

"I didn't," said her brothers.

"Did-did," said the baby.

"Please wait for me, Daddy," she cried.

She ran upstairs again. This time she looked in her closet. The shoes were not there.

She ran downstairs and looked in the hall closet. No shoes.

"Sorry. You can't go without shoes," said Daddy. "Better hunt them up. You would save yourself a lot of bother if you put your shoes away when you kicked them off." And he went off without her.

Eva Mae stopped trying to find her shoes. "Certainly they will turn up tomorrow," she said to herself.

The next day was Sunday. She wore her
new black shoes to church. After dinner,
Mama said, "You may not wear your good
shoes to play in."

So Eva Mae went barefooted. She found
some good puddles to splash in. And she didn't
even try to find her shoes. "Surely someone
will find them for me by tomorrow," she said to
herself.

Before supper Mama called Eva Mae to her.
"Sunshine girl, you do not seem to care
if you find your shoes or if you don't. You do
not seem to care if you obey me or not. You
are not trying to find your school shoes
because you think someone else will surely
find them.

"You may not wear your Sunday shoes to
school. If you cannot find your school shoes,
you will stay home tomorrow. I will tell Miss

Kline you had to stay home because you lost your shoes."

"Oh, no, Mama!" cried Eva Mae. "What will Miss Kline think? All the children will laugh at me when I go back to school. I have looked for my shoes, but I can't find them." Tears stood in her eyes.

"Well, you must look again," said Mama. "Remember what I told you. You must learn to take care of your shoes. Maybe staying home from school will help you to obey me. See what a bother it is to everyone when you lose your shoes? Maybe it will help you to put your shoes in a safe place when you kick them off. Now, go look again. They surely are somewhere."

And Eva Mae did look. She looked upstairs and downstairs. She looked in all the rooms and in all the closets.

She asked, "Did anyone see my shoes?"

"I didn't," said Daddy and Mama.

"I didn't," said her sisters and brothers.

"Did-did," said the baby.

Eva Mae sat on her bed, ready to cry. She could not find her shoes. She could not go to school tomorrow.

Suddenly, she thought of something Daddy had often said: "When we are in trouble, we should ask God to help us. He cares for us." Why hadn't she thought of that before? She surely was in trouble now!

Eva Mae slid down beside her bed. "Dear God, will You please tell me where my shoes are? You certainly can see them right now. Help me to think where I left them. Help me after this to obey Mama and put my shoes in a safe place every time. Thank You. Amen."

Eva Mae went downstairs. "Mama, I haven't found my shoes. I have looked everywhere. But I asked God to help me think where they are. And I asked Him to help me obey you after this too. I'm sorry I didn't obey you. Lost shoes certainly are a nuisance.

"Now I am going to sit on this chair and think about when I had them last. I'm going to think about where I took them off.

"I know I had them on Friday. It was raining and I wore my boots to school. We splashed in the puddles on the way home."

Suddenly Eva Mae's big blue eyes got bigger. Her mouth fell open. "Mama!" she squealed. "Now I know just where they are!"

She jumped off the chair and ran out the door. In no time she was back with a brown boot in each hand.

"In my boots. In my boots," she sang. "I just slipped out of my shoes and left them in my boots. And now I can go to school tomorrow!" Then she began to cry.

Mama put her arm around her. "This is no time to cry, Sunshine Girl. This is the time to thank the Lord for His goodness to little girls who pray."

Eva Mae brushed her tears away with both hands. "I know, Mama. Isn't it **something** how God knew where my shoes were all the time? But He didn't tell me till I asked Him! Now I know He will help me take care of my shoes after this, because I asked Him to do that too."

–*Elva E. Leaman*

Eva Mae had two sets of five little brothers who also liked to run free.

Five Little Brothers

Five little brothers set out together
    to journey the livelong day,
In a curious carriage all made of leather
    They hurried away, away!
One big brother and three quite small,
    And one wee fellow, no size at all.

The carriage was dark and none too roomy,
    And they could not move about.
The five little brothers grew very gloomy,
    And the wee one began to pout,
Till the biggest one whispered, "What do you say—
    Let's leave the carriage and run away!"

11

So out they scampered, the five together,
    And off and away they sped!
When someone found that carriage of leather,
    Oh, my! how she shook her head.
'Twas her little boy's shoe, as everyone knows,
    And the five little brothers were five little toes.

— Ella Wheeler Wilcox

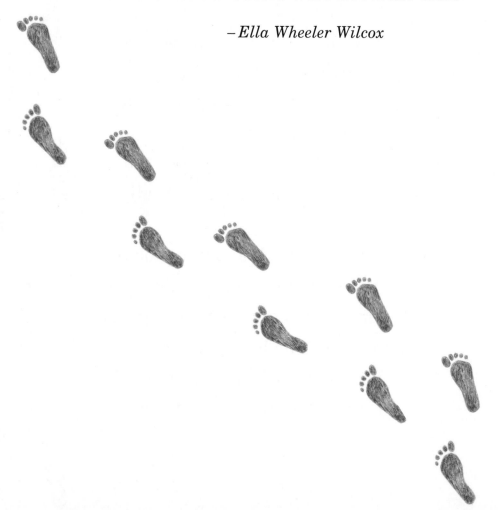

Eva Mae lost her smile along with her shoes.
She found her smile when she found her shoes.

Lost and Found

Lost! a very precious thing;
    A sunny little smile.
Although we've missed it but an hour,
    It seems a long, long while.
The last time that we saw it
    Was on Mary Josephine;
She wore it last at breakfast,
    Since then it's not been seen.

It shone just like a sunbeam
    On the little maiden's face;
Two merry, twinkling dimples kept
    The pretty thing in place;
I fear someone has stolen it;
    I can't think where it's gone;
I only know, without it, all
    The household is forlorn.

Oh, joy! Oh, joy; I've found it.
     You never could guess where,
For I had looked and hunted
     Under sofa, bed, and chair;
Had searched in every closet,
     Had peered behind the screen,
Had sat me down discouraged
     With Mary Josephine.

A frown was on her forehead,
     Her lips were pursed up tight;
I couldn't keep from sighing;
     At such a dismal sight;
But then from eyes and rosy lips
     That precious smile peeped out!
It had been hiding all the time
     Behind that little pout!

                    –Author Unknown

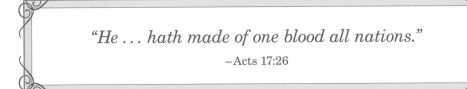

"He . . . hath made of one blood all nations."
—Acts 17:26

The Red Children

How are you like the children in this story?

Hundreds of years ago there were no white people in this country. There were no towns, farms, or highways. There were only deep woods and wide, grassy **plains.**

The people who lived here had black hair, dark eyes, and dark skin. The white men who came to this country from across the ocean said they had red skin. But it was not really red.

These dark-skinned people were called

Indians, but none of them had ever seen India. Today we call these people Native Americans.

The Indians were strong and brave. The men hunted and fished for food. The women did all the other work.

There were different **tribes** of Indians. Some tribes lived in the North. Some lived in the South. Some lived in the East, and some in the West.

These tribes were different in many ways, just as you and I are different from people who live across the ocean.

They dressed in different kinds of clothes. Each tribe spoke a different language. They lived in different kinds of **shelters** for houses.

One kind of house was the **tepee.** It was made of long poles tied together at the top.

The bottom ends of the poles were spread in a big circle. Animal skins covered the poles. A hole in the top of the tepee let out the smoke of the cook fire. The cook fire was built on the ground in the center of the tepee.

The Indians went in and out through a flap left open in the side. Many Indians painted pictures on their tepees.

The **wickiup** was another kind of house. It was almost like the tepee.

When Indians were on the move, they needed shelter for just a day or two. They did not want to spend time making a good tepee, so they made a wickiup.

They used poles as for the tepee, but covered them with grass, brush, or mats woven from reeds. A wickiup could be put up and taken down quickly. It was a quick way to make a shelter.

Another kind of house was the **wigwam.**

It, too, was round. The poles in the frame were bent over like an upside-down bowl. The Indians covered the frame with bark, grass mats, or skins.

Sometimes a tepee is called a wigwam. But they really are different kinds of shelters.

In the Southwest, some Indians made homes by digging out rooms in the soft rock of a huge cliff. Some homes were made of **sandstone** blocks held together with mud **mortar.** These Indians were called **cliff dwellers.** Sometimes they added rooms made of stones or mud bricks dried in the sun. They used ladders to reach the rooms higher up on the cliff.

Cliff dwellers, as well as Indians of other tribes, hunted with bows and arrows. They made arrowheads and tools of stone.

One day, an Indian was teaching his son

how to shoot with a bow and arrow. To see
how high he could shoot, the boy placed a long
arrow on his bow. He pulled the string back as
far as he could and let it fly.

The arrow went up and up and up in the
air. It went out of sight. It went so high that
they did not see it fall to the ground.

The Indian father said his son had shot a
hole in the sky. After this, he always called his
son Hole-in-the-Sky.

Hole-in-the-Sky had a sister who had weak
eyes. She always looked sleepy, so her father
and mother named her Sleepy-Eye.

Indian boys liked to play games. One of
these games was called *Hunting the Buffalo*. It
was very much like *Fox and Hounds*. The boys
who were hunters went into a tepee. They
must not see which way the buffalo went.

The boy who was the buffalo ran off into

the woods. He tried to hide his tracks so the
hunters could not follow him.

In *Fox and Hounds*, the
fox drops bits of paper as
he goes along. The hounds
follow the fox by finding
the bits of paper.

Indian boys did not need bits of paper. The hunters stayed in the tepee until the buffalo had a good start. Then they started after him. They were such good hunters they could see where the buffalo had run. They could see his footprints in soft soil. They could see where grass was bent down.

They could see a leaf his foot had turned over. The buffalo tried to stay so far ahead that the hunters never spied him running.

Hole-in-the-Sky always liked to be one of the buffaloes. He was a good runner, and it often took the other boys all day to catch him.

Hole-in-the-Sky also liked to go with his friends to fight a wild bees' nest. Wild bees store honey in the hollow trunks of trees.

Before starting, the boys painted their faces. They stuck some feathers in their hair. Then they went through the woods until they came to a bee tree. They could see bees going in and out of a hole high up on the trunk.

When everything was ready, they ran toward the tree with wild cries. They beat on it with sticks and threw stones at the hole.

Bees knew how to sting then as well as they do now. They buzzed out to **protect** their home.

Sometimes a great many bees would fly at one boy. He would have to take to his heels.

The only way to stop the bees from stinging was to jump into deep water. The boys did not mind this for they all were good swimmers.

No matter how many bee stings they got, Indian boys did not cry. They thought that brave boys never cried.

Sleepy-Eye never had much time to play games. She had to help her mother work.

When her mother went away, Sleepy-Eye took care of her little brother. She enjoyed doing that. He was a good baby.

He was tied on a flat piece of wood covered with skin. Sleepy-Eye could hang this cradle up in the tepee or on a tree. Then she played with her dolls.

Hole-in-the-Sky had made the dolls for her. They were pieces of wood cut in the shape of people. They were covered with skin. Horsehair was used for hair, and the eyes were beads.

Whenever their father came home from hunting, Hole-in-the-Sky and Sleepy-Eye liked to hear the stories he told. The best time of all was the long winter evenings. Then the whole family sat around a bright fire in the tepee and listened to his hunting stories.

–Author Unknown

*Do you think Sleepy-Eye's mother sang
this lullaby to Baby Brother when
she rocked him to sleep at night?*

Rock-a-by, Hush-a-by, Little Papoose

Rock-a-by, hush-a-by, little papoose,
    The stars come into the sky,
The whip-po'-will's crying, the daylight is dying,
    The river runs murmuring by.

The pine trees are slumbering, little papoose;
    The squirrel has gone to his nest,
The robins are sleeping, the mother bird's keeping
    The little ones warm with her breast.

Then hush-a-by, rock-a-by, little papoose,
    You sail on the river of dreams;
Our God dearly loves you, and watches above you
    Till time when the morning light gleams.

– Charles Myali

Most boys would enjoy playing Hunting the Buffalo. *They would enjoy the excitement of fighting a wild bees' nest. They would enjoy sitting at a fire in a tepee and listening to their father tell hunting stories.*

Hole-in-the-Sky enjoyed all these things, not because he was an Indian, but because he was a happy boy who loved his friends and family.

What does this poem say it takes to be happy?

Happy Hearts

Happiness does not depend
On being white- or yellow-skinned,
    Or red
        or black
           or brown.

Happy hearts can laugh
and sing,
Say "Thank You, God"
in everything,
And smile
instead
of frown.

Happy hearts are full of love
For others, and for God above,
Who sends
rich blessings
down.

– Merna B. Shank

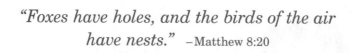

"Foxes have holes, and the birds of the air have nests." —Matthew 8:20

All Kinds of Houses

What do you like about Uncle Mike?

Philip and Dottie called Uncle Mike their "outdoor uncle." When he came to visit, he spent more time **roaming** outdoors than he did inside.

He went out in the early morning while everyone was asleep. "That is the best time to see and hear God's **creatures,**" he said.

Often he was the last one in at night. He liked to lie out in the yard after dark.

He liked to look at the stars and listen to the night creatures.

"You miss a lot if you come inside when the sun goes down," he said.

Uncle Mike had come to stay for a week. Philip and Dottie had made big plans.

"We will climb the mountain," said Philip.

"We will go roaming in the woods," said Dottie.

"We will fish in the pond," said Philip.

"We will show him the creek," said Dottie.

"We will roam all over the place and he will tell us something about everything we see. That's what I like about Uncle Mike," said Philip. "He knows everything."

On the first day they went on a hike. But a big rain came up. They **dashed** for the house, and made it just in time.

"I'm glad we didn't get wet," said Philip.

"It is nice to have a house to run to when it rains."

"Where do all the birds and animals go when it rains?" asked Dottie. "Do they have houses where they stay warm and dry?"

"Some do and some don't," said Uncle Mike. "Some don't mind getting wet. Some die if they don't stay wet. I think God made animals and birds so they know how to find or make a house if they need one. Isn't that **marvelous**?"

"What I think is marvelous," said Philip, "is how birds and bees find their way back to their houses. They can roam over the hills and fields for miles. Yet they can get back to their houses without any roads or signs or anything."

"Let's see how many kinds of houses we can think of," said Uncle Mike.

"Holes are one kind," said Dottie.

"Bluebirds and woodpeckers live in holes."

"So do **groundhogs** and **muskrats**," put in Philip. "And **crayfish** that live in the wet part of the cornfield."

"Did you ever see those fine webs with a

hole in the middle for the spider?" asked Uncle Mike.

"Oh, yes. I saw one of those in the yard," said Dottie. "And snakes and earthworms live in holes."

"Foxes have holes, and the birds of the air have nests," said Uncle Mike.

"Jesus said that, didn't He?" asked Philip.

"Yes, He did. Do you know any other creatures besides birds that have nests?"

"I know some," cried Philip. "Mice and squirrels do. A mouse nest is made of soft things, like rags and paper. The babies are way down in it all snug and warm. And a squirrel's nest looks like a big ball of leaves in the top of the tree. I have often seen a squirrel dash up a tree and into one of those leaf nests."

"That's right. And can you think of a house made of paper?"

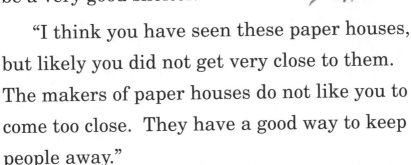

"A paper house!" cried Dottie. "Who would make a house of paper? Paper wouldn't be a very good shelter."

"I think you have seen these paper houses, but likely you did not get very close to them. The makers of paper houses do not like you to come too close. They have a good way to keep people away."

"Oh, now I know," cried Philip. "You are talking about wasps and **hornets** and yellow jackets. They are the creatures that make paper houses.

"Dottie, you know that big hornet nest the teacher has at school. It is bigger than a basketball."

"Yes, and those little gray wasp nests in the old henhouse. Philip likes to knock them down, but I stay away from them."

"Isn't it funny how a tiny little yellow jacket can make big people run?" said Uncle Mike.

"Where do wasps get all that gray paper?" asked Dottie.

"They make it," said Uncle Mike. "They chew up wood or plant stems. When they spit it out, it dries like paper."

"Just think how many mouthfuls it took to make that hornet nest at school!" said Philip. "I wouldn't want to be a hornet or wasp and chew up a lot of wood and stems to make my house."

"Neither would I. I would rather move into a house that someone else made," said Uncle Mike.

"Who does that?" asked Dottie.

"The **hermit crab**. He finds a snail shell on the beach and backs into it. That becomes his house.

"If the snail still lives in the shell, the hermit crab pulls it out and eats it. Then he takes over the shell for his house."

"Ugh!" said Dottie. "What a way to get a house!"

"I would rather be a turtle and have my house with me all the time," said Philip. "I'd never have to go home. I'd never have to dash for the house when it began to rain. I'd just pull in my head and feet and close up my front door and be safe and dry."

Dottie shook her head. "That is all right for a turtle. But I want a house where there is room for other people. If you were a turtle, where would Uncle Mike stay when he came to visit?"

Philip laughed. "I didn't think about that," he said. "I guess God made everything to fit the kind of house He planned for it."

−Ruth K. Hobbs

Which of the houses in these poems do you think would be the safest? Which would be the warmest? Which would be the most fun to live in?

The House of the Mouse

The house of the mouse is a wee little house,
  A green little house in the grass,
Which big clumsy folk may hunt
    and may poke
      And still never see as they pass
        this sweet little,
          neat little,
            wee little,
              green little,
                cuddle-down,
                  hide-away
                    house in the grass.

– Lucy Sprague Mitchell

The Jolly Woodchuck

The woodchuck's very, very fat,
But doesn't care a pin for that.
When nights are long and the snow is deep,
Down in his hole he lies asleep.
Under the earth is a warm little room
The drowsy woodchuck calls his home.
Rolls of fat and fur surround him,
With all his children curled around him,
Snout to snout and tail to tail,
He never awakes in the wildest gale:
When icicles snap and the north wind blows
He snores in his sleep and rubs his nose.

– Marion Edey and Dorothy Grider

What Happened
in the Night

Last night I swung till twilight time
Beneath the big oak tree.
I swung 'way up, I swung 'way down.
I swung to the right and turned around.
And not a single soul I found.
     So the swing belonged to me.

This morn I went to swing again
Beneath the big oak tree.
But a spider slim was
    already there.
He had spun a web
    beyond compare.
To take the swing I
    didn't dare.
    For the swing was
      his, you see.

—Author Unknown

The Woodpecker

The woodpecker pecked out a little round hole
And made him a house in the telephone pole.
One day when I watched he poked out his head,
And he had on a hood and a collar of red.

When the streams of rain pour out of the sky,
And the sparkles of lightning go flashing by,
And the big, big wheels of thunder roll,
He can snuggle back in the telephone pole.

– Elizabeth Madox Roberts

Four Thousand for Dinner

Why were so many people following Jesus?

1. In those days the **multitude** being very great, and having nothing to eat, Jesus called his **disciples** unto him, and saith unto them,
2. I have **compassion** on the multitude, because they have now been with me three days, and have nothing to eat:
3. And if I send them away **fasting** to their own houses, they will **faint** by the way: for **divers** of them came from far.
4. And his disciples answered him, From **whence** can a man **satisfy** these men with bread here in the **wilderness**?
5. And he asked them, How many **loaves** have ye? And they said, Seven.
6. And he **commanded** the people to sit down on the ground: and he took the seven loaves, and gave thanks, and **brake**, and gave to his disciples to set before them; and they did set them before the people.

7. And they had a few small fishes: and he blessed, and commanded to set them also before them.

8. So they did eat, and were filled: and they took up of the broken meat that was left seven baskets.

9. And they that had eaten were about four thousand: and he sent them away.

– Mark 8:1-9

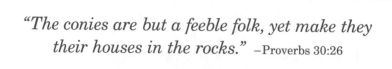

"The conies are but a feeble folk, yet make they their houses in the rocks." –Proverbs 30:26

To Save Their Lives

Can you think of another way some of God's creatures protect themselves?

"I have an idea," said Philip as he and Dottie and Uncle Mike went out the back gate.

"Yesterday I thought of something when we talked about wasp nests. Dottie said she stays away when I knock them down. She is afraid they will sting her. Stinging is the way wasps protect themselves. Let's keep our eyes open for other ways God's creatures protect themselves."

"I see a way," Dottie cried, looking up. There in the blue sky a big bird floated around and around on wide black wings. "Flying is the way birds keep safe. What could get that bird way up there?"

"Are birds the only creatures who protect themselves by flying?" asked Uncle Mike.

"No. There goes something that isn't a bird," cried Philip. A grasshopper popped up from the path. It sped into the weeds on black-and-yellow wings.

"Stings and wings," sang Dottie. "They are two ways God's creatures protect themselves."

"We have seen two kinds of creatures with wings—birds and insects," said Uncle Mike. "Does anything else use wings?"

"I have heard of flying fish," said Philip. "Their wings are not true wings, but they do help the fish to get away from its **enemies**."

"I know of an animal that flies," put in Uncle Mike.

"An animal! Oh, yes, the flying squirrel," said Dottie.

"No, that is not what I am thinking of."

"Anyway, a flying squirrel does not really fly," said Philip. "It doesn't even have wings. It just glides like a paper airplane."

"That is right. The animal I am thinking of has wings and really flies."

"You mean an animal like a tiger or a cow has wings and floats in the air like that bird up there?" asked Dottie, her eyes big.

Uncle Mike laughed. "I didn't say it was like a tiger or a cow. I just said it was an animal. I won't tell you what it is until we go in for breakfast. Maybe you will think of it by then.

"But for now, let's think about that

grasshopper. He does something else that keeps him safe."

"I know what it is," said Philip. "He hops. Grasshoppers can hop so far and fast you can hardly catch them. Rabbits and kangaroos hop too. So do frogs and toads."

"Grasshoppers do three things that keep them safe. From me at least," said Dottie, making a face. "I don't like that ugly brown juice they spit on you when you catch them."

"Many creatures have more than one way to protect themselves," Uncle Mike said.

"A rabbit can jump. It can run. What else can it do?"

"Well, I know a rabbit can kick and scratch with its hind legs," said Philip. "I found that out when I tried to catch our pet rabbit and put him back in the pen."

"Stop a minute!" said Uncle Mike, putting up his hand. "Right now I see a rabbit. He is protecting himself in another way."

"A rabbit?" asked Philip. "Where?"

"Look for it. I am not going to tell you yet. Your eyes are as good as mine. Just stand still and use your eyes."

Philip and Dottie stood still and looked all around. But they did not see a rabbit.

"Uncle Mike, please tell us where it is," whispered Dottie.

"Not yet. I want you to learn how to use your own eyes. Let's walk on slowly. If you can't see it pretty soon, then I will tell you."

Slowly, slowly, step by step they went on down the dusty path. The children looked and looked, but saw nothing.

"Stop," said Uncle Mike quietly. "Now look on the right side of the path, there by that rock. Can you see it?"

The children looked. Dottie gave a little gasp.

"Oh, a baby rabbit!"

"He is only eight or ten feet away," said Philip softly.

They stood very still until the little rabbit took three slow hops out of sight into the bushes.

"That rabbit did not hop or run or kick or scratch. What kept him safe?"

"**Camouflage**!" cried Philip. "He was brown, like the dusty grass. And he just sat still. We would have gone right by him if you had not seen him, Uncle Mike."

"You are right. Camouflage is the way lots of God's creatures **escape** being caught.

"But there goes your mother's bell. That means breakfast is ready. We must go back."

"We just got started," said Dottie. "Could we go after breakfast and look for more?"

"Yes, if your mother doesn't need you to

help her. How many ways have we talked about so far?"

"Stinging and flying and running," said Dottie.

"Hopping and kicking and scratching, and camouflage," said Philip. "That is seven ways animals protect themselves."

"And spitting ugly brown juice. That makes eight," said Uncle Mike with a laugh.

A little later as they ate breakfast, Dottie said, "Now tell us about the animal that has wings and protects itself by flying."

"I know you have seen this animal," said Uncle Mike. "You just haven't thought of it. The animal is the bat."

"Of course!" said Philip. "I knew that."

"I did too," said Dottie. "I just didn't think. But who would want to catch a *bat*? Not I!"

–Ruth K. Hobbs

How did the bunny in this poem protect itself?

A Story in the Snow

This morning, as I walked to school
　　Across the fluffy snow,
I came upon a bunny's tracks—
　　A jumping, zigzag row.

He must have hurried very fast,
　　For here and there I saw
Along his jerky, winding trail
　　The print of Rover's paw!

I set my lunch pail on the snow
　　And stood there very still.
For only Rover's clumsy tracks
　　Led down the little hill.

Then suddenly I thought I heard
A rustling sound close by;
And there within a grassy clump
Shone Bunny's twinkling eye!

– Pearl Riggs Crouch

What was the flying star this child found? Have you ever caught this kind of flying star?

The Flying Stars

Mother, I caught a little star,
    But then I let it go;
I let it go again, because
    The poor thing
      struggled so.

I caught it safely in my hand,
    Down in the marshes, where
Hundreds have fallen from the sky,
    And now are sparkling there.

And though the meadow is so wet,
    Yet they are still as bright
As when so high up in the sky,
    I see them shine at night.

Their little lights blinked off and on,
    Just how I cannot say.
The one I had lit up my hand,
    Before it flew away.

And, Mother, I have found out now,
    Books teach what is not right;
They say the shining little stars
    Are monstrous globes of light.

But now I know it is not so,
    For all that books may say;
They're small black bugs with yellow lights
    And wings to fly away.

–Author Unknown

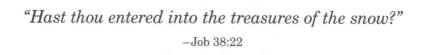

"Hast thou entered into the treasures of the snow?"

–Job 38:22

Snow Camel for Beth

*What did Joel do to keep himself from
thinking about outdoor fun?*

It was Saturday. Mama was in the kitchen
baking. Joel and Beth were playing a fast
game of **Chinese checkers**.

Joel tried not to look out the window. He
did not want to see the blue sky and the
sunshine on the snow.

Joel liked to play Chinese checkers with
Beth. But not on Saturday. Not when there
was snow on the ground. Not when the ice

on the pond might have frozen thick enough for skating.

So he played Chinese checkers and tried not to think about snow fun and ice skating. He tried to **imagine** how Beth must feel with her leg in that stiff, white cast. He **glanced** at that stiff cast as they played. He looked at the **crutches** lying on the floor by her chair. He tried not to look out the window.

He knew Beth's days were long when he was in school. He knew she was happy when Saturday came and he could do things to **amuse** her.

Just then the doorbell gave a fast blink-blonk. Joel went to the door. It was Matt.

"Get your skates, Joel. The ice has frozen thick enough. Daddy checked it. It's as slick as glass! I imagine the other boys are already there."

"I'd really like to, but ..." Joel glanced back at Beth with her broken leg up on a chair.

"You go on, Joel," Beth said. "Don't miss skating for me. I can amuse myself."

Joel went out on the porch with Matt. He shut the door behind him.

"I want to go, Matt. But I told Mama I'd do things to amuse Beth today."

"That's too bad," said Matt. He thought a bit, then said, "I know what! How about if we would ..." Matt kept on talking, but he spoke very quietly so Beth would not hear.

"That's a great idea," said Joel. "Let's do it. I'll ask Mama if I can go skating after we do that. I imagine she'll let me."

The boys came into the house. Beth said, "I really want you to go, Joel. It would be fun if I could see the pond from here, but that's all right. I'll amuse myself with something. We can play Chinese checkers tonight."

"I must ask Mama," said Joel. He went into the kitchen.

Soon the boys went out with their skates. Beth glanced out at the blue sky and the sunshine on the snowy yard. Her face was sad.

She was glad the boys had gone skating. But she could imagine the fun she was missing in the snow and on the frozen pond.

Then she thought she heard a laugh. It came from outside the other window. The window was shut, but Beth was sure she heard someone laugh. She couldn't imagine who would be laughing out there in the side yard.

Beth picked up her crutches. She got up and hopped to the window.

There in the side yard were Joel and Matt.

They were trying to put a head on a big snow camel. They had made a snow camel kneeling on the ground.

The neck of the camel was too thin to hold the head. It kept falling off. That was why they were laughing so hard.

Beth began to laugh too. She put up the window and stuck out her head.

"Joel," she called. "I thought you two had gone skating. Did you make that funny camel for me?"

"Yes. We thought you needed someone to talk to when we were gone. But this old camel doesn't seem to want a head," Joel called back.

"His neck is too thin. Bring me some more snow," said Matt.

Soon the camel's neck was as thick as a post. Then the boys put on the head. This time it stuck.

The boys stepped back and looked at the snow camel. How they all did laugh!

"If it didn't have a hump you would just have to imagine what kind of animal it is," said Matt. "It does not look much like a camel with that straight, stiff neck."

"I think it's marvelous," cried Beth. "Thank you for making it for me.

"Now while you go skating, I will make camels for you."

"What kind of camels can you make?" asked Joel.

"I'm not telling. Just wait and see," said Beth. "Matt, you must stop in and see them before you go home. I'll make one for each of you."

"All right, I will," said Matt.

The boys picked up their skates. They patted the snow camel's hump. They waved to Beth's smiling face in the window. Then they went off to the pond.

Much, much later, Joel and Matt came home. Beth met them at the door on her crutches.

"We came for our camels," they said. "We can't imagine what kind they are." They glanced around. "Where are they?"

"Come with me," said Beth, hopping out to the kitchen.

There on the table lay three big cookie camels. Mama stood there with a jug of hot chocolate.

"These are for two boys who made me very happy today," Beth said.

The boys sat down at the table.

"Your camels look more like camels than the snow camel does," said Joel, as he bit off his camel's head.

"These taste better than ours would," said Matt, as he bit off his camel's hump.

"I had the most fun making them," said Beth, as she bit off her camel's legs.

And Mama could not tell which child had the happiest face as they all drank their hot chocolate.

−Ruth K. Hobbs

If you live where you can't make snowmen, you may need
to ask someone what a sugar bucket is. Or can you guess?

The Snowman

Our snowman's nearly finished
   And we have had great fun;
Mother's coming out to look
   As soon as he is done.

His bright black eyes are bits of coal,
   His scarf belongs to Ted,
His hat's a sugar bucket
   We found out in the shed.

He has real buttons on his coat,
   A broomstick in his hand;
He stands up tall and straight,
As though he owned the land.

– Francis Frost

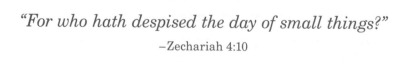

> *"For who hath despised the day of small things?"*
> –Zechariah 4:10

Money in His Pocket

Was Pablo happier when he had money in his
pocket or when his money was in screws?

Pablo lived in **Mexico**. That is the country south of the United States. He was six years old. His church stood at the end of the street. It had stone walls and red tiles for the roof.

The church was new. It was so new that it was not **finished** yet. Only half the tiles were on the roof. Instead of a door, there was a big hole in the wall where the door would go.

Until the church was finished, Pablo had

to go to Sunday school in the house of a neighbor. So many children came that some of them could not get in. They had to stand outside and look through the window. Pablo could squeeze inside. He was thin and did not take up much space at all.

Pablo's father was dead. His mother worked hard washing clothes to make a little money. Pablo had three patches on his white cotton pants. The brim of his straw hat was broken. On weekdays he had nothing to eat but beans and corn. Sometimes there wasn't enough food to fill him up.

On Saturday Pablo's mother counted out ten **centavos** from her washing money.

"Pablo," she said, "here are ten centavos to buy sweet rolls for Sunday dinner."

Every Sunday Pablo had two sweet rolls. How he looked forward to that treat! All week he thought about those two sweet rolls.

Pablo put the ten centavos into his pocket. He set out for the bakery. He had money in his pocket. Money to **jingle**! Money to spend!

Pablo felt rich. He jingled his ten centavos all the way down the street.

When he came to the new church, he stopped to watch the men working. He saw a big door standing against the front wall.

"Good morning," he said to his friend, who was boss of the job. "Why don't you hang the door where it belongs?"

"We can't hang the door until we can buy the **hinges** and the screws," said his friend.

"Does it take a lot of money to build a church?"

"Yes, Pablo, it does. But if we all give something, we will have enough."

Pablo had money in his pocket. Money to jingle. Money to give.

"Can you buy something for the church with ten centavos?" he asked.

The boss smiled. "Ten centavos will buy screws for the door," he said.

Pablo reached into his pocket and took out his money. "Then take my ten. I want to help build the new church!"

Pablo had no sweet rolls for his dinner that Sunday. But he didn't mind being a little hungry.

At last the church was finished.

And now, when Pablo goes in and out, he stops to look up at the hinges that hold the door.

"Those are my screws up there," he says to his mother with a broad happy smile.

And together they watch the big door swing open to all the people.

– Dorothy Ballard

"The angel of the LORD encampeth round about them that fear him, and delivereth them." –Psalm 34:7

Seen Through the Tent Door

Why did the Indians want to hear what David had come to tell them?

"Don't go, David," begged his friend.

"We are **positive** the Indians will kill you," said another one.

"We will never see you again," said someone else.

"What good can you do if the Indians kill you?"

"Stay here where you are safe. Preach to the white people. They need salvation too."

No one wanted David to go.

The young man shook his head. "I am positive the **Holy Spirit** of God wants me to go to the Indians. They need **salvation** as well as we. They do not know about Jesus. Jesus died for them too. I must go."

"But the Indians hate white men. They will kill you before you can tell them about Jesus," said one.

"Indians have their own gods. They will not want the white man's God anyway," said another.

"Our God is not only the white man's God," said David. "He is also the Indians' God. Jesus died for the Indians too. They need salvation, but they do not know it. I must go and tell them. I am positive that is what God wants me to do."

David **Brainerd** lived in America long ago. God had called David to go to a big Indian village and tell them about Jesus. The village was a long way off.

David rolled up his small sleeping tent. He put it on his back. He said good-bye to his sad friends. Off he went through the thick forest.

There were no roads through the forest. David had to find his own way. He walked on Indian trails when he could find them.

He walked five days. Then he saw he was **approaching** the Indian village. He stopped, well out of sight. He set up his little sleeping tent. Then he went inside and kneeled down to pray.

The Holy Spirit had led him to the village. But now David wanted to ask God the best way to make friends with the Indians. He wanted to ask God the best way to begin telling them the story of salvation. He wanted to ask God to take care of him. "I will pray until I am positive what the Holy Spirit wants me to do next," he said to himself.

Long before David Brainerd had gotten near the Indian village, the Indians knew he was coming. **Scouts** who watched all the trails had seen him approaching. They had run swiftly to the village. They told everyone a white man was coming.

The Indians said, "We must kill him! White men have brought only **evil** to our land. This man is up to no good. We will kill him as soon as he gets to the village!"

The Indian scouts went back to the trail. They hid. They watched David approaching with the little pack on his back.

They saw him stop. They watched him

take off his pack. They watched him put up the tent and go inside. Then all was silent.

The Indians watched and watched. Nothing happened. No sound came from the tent. What could the white man be doing all this time? Was he planning some evil thing to do to them?

Silently, as only Indians can move, they

approached. Then they heard the man talking.
Who was in the tent with him? They had seen
only one man. Who could he be talking to?

At last they moved near enough to look
through the tent door.

They saw the young white man on his
knees. His back was to the door. His head was
bowed over his hands. His eyes were shut and
he was talking.

Then the Indians saw something else.
They saw a thick, ugly rattlesnake slide
silently under the edge of the tent. With
mouth wide open, it approached, ready to
strike the neck of the kneeling man.

But suddenly, as if hearing the voice of its
Creator, the snake stopped. The Indians saw
it drop its ugly head and slip out of the tent as
silently as it had come.

The scouts, too, stepped quietly away

from the tent. Their eyes were wide with wonder as they ran swiftly back to the village. They told everyone what they had seen through the tent door.

"The white man's head was bowed. His eyes were shut. He was talking to the Great Spirit," they said. "The Great Spirit protected him from the evil snake that rattles. The Great Spirit is taking care of this man. When he comes we must listen to what he says."

David Brainerd prayed and waited to learn what God wanted him to do. He knew nothing about the snake or the scouts who looked into his tent.

At last he felt certain he knew what God wanted him to do. He took his Bible and approached the village.

To his surprise, he saw the Indians coming to meet him. They wanted to hear what he had come to tell them.

David told the Indians about God's love for them. He told them the story of salvation. He became their friend. Only then did they tell him what the scouts had seen through the tent door.

—Author Unknown

"Wisdom is the principal thing; therefore get wisdom."

—Proverbs 4:7

The Boy Who Determined to Learn

Why did Saddhu put up with the mean rich boys?

Saddhu lived in a little hut in the far-away country of India. The hut had a grass roof and a hard dirt floor.

His father and mother worked long and hard to buy rice to eat and **kerosene** for their one lamp.

Saddhu had a job away from home. But at night he needed a light to read by, for Saddhu had been taught to read by an old neighbor who had once worked for an American missionary.

Every evening Saddhu would **ignore** how tired he was. He would light the kerosene lamp and read far into the night. He studied every book he could get his hands on. "I want to learn about everything," he said. "Most of all I want to go to school."

In our country, all children must go to school. It was not that way in India. There, only rich children could go to school.

Saddhu knew this, but still he dreamed of going to school. He was **determined** to learn somehow. Often he would beg his father, "Please let me stop work and go to school."

Always his father said, "Where could you go to school? You have no **business** at the school in town. Only rich boys are allowed to go to the town school."

But Saddhu kept begging. He kept dreaming of being able to go to school sometime. He kept reading everything he could get his hands on. He made sure there was kerosene for the lamp at night. He **memorized** everything in every book he read. He still was determined to learn.

Then one day his father said, "You may go and talk to the teacher in the town school. You may ask if you can go to school there. But do not get your hopes up. The school is for rich boys. You are too poor. The other boys would not want the likes of you. The teacher would ignore you."

Saddhu put on clean clothes. He walked through the hot India sun down the hot dusty road to the school in town.

He rapped at the open window. The teacher came and put out his head.

"What do you want, little **beggar**?" he

asked. "You don't belong here."

"May I please come to your school?" asked Saddhu.

"You!" cried the teacher. "This school is not for beggars. You have no business here. Do you have money?"

Saddhu shook his head sadly. "No, I do not have money. But I can read. I have memorized many things. Would you please let me come?"

The teacher looked at Saddhu as if he did not believe him. He said, "You are not allowed to come to this school. But if you are determined to learn, you may sit outside under the window. You may listen to me teach if you can learn anything that way."

Then he threw some old books out the window and went back to the rich boys.

With joy Saddhu picked up the books, sat down, and began to read.

Every school day after that, Saddhu sat in the hot sand in the hot India sun under the window. The shade of a nearby tree looked so cool. But he could not hear the teacher unless he sat close under the window. Saddhu learned everything in all the books the teacher threw out.

The rich boys in the school did not make friends with Saddhu. They thought he had no business sitting under the window. Sometimes they ignored him. At other times they made fun of him. They threw trash out on him. Sometimes when the teacher was not looking they reached out with a stick and **rapped** him on the head.

But Saddhu did not mind that. He was too happy reading and learning all that was in the old books. As long as he had something to read, it was easy to ignore everything around him.

One day the School **Inspector** came. It was this man's business to see how well the children were learning. He rapped at the door and went in.

He listened to the rich boys read. He asked them many questions about what was in their books. Then he asked, "Why is that boy out there in the hot sun under the window?"

"Oh, he is too poor to come to this school," said the teacher. "I am not allowed to have him in here with the rich boys. But he is determined to learn. I throw old books out to him, and he listens to me through the window. But I am sure he has not learned much that way. He is too poor to come to school like the other boys."

"You should not ignore any boy who wants to learn that badly," said the School Inspector. "Bring the boy to me. I will see if he has learned anything sitting out there."

Saddhu came into the schoolhouse. The Inspector gave him a book.

For a long time the Inspector listened to Saddhu read. He asked him many hard questions. Saddhu could answer them all.

At last the Inspector stood in front of the school. He had Saddhu stand beside him.

He said, "This poor boy who learned by sitting under your window can read better than anyone in this school. He knows more than any of the rest of you."

How surprised the rich boys were. How happy Saddhu was. The teacher was happy too. After that, he gave Saddhu good, new books to read.

Saddhu still was not allowed to go to the rich boys' school. But he did not care. He had all the books he wanted.

Before long, missionaries started a new school in the town. They did not ignore poor children. Anyone who wanted to learn could go to that school. Saddhu was there on the very first day.

In the new school he learned about God and Jesus and their love for him. He learned to read the Bible. The first verse he memorized was John 3:16.

Saddhu studied hard. He read everything he could get his hands on.

Years later if you had visited that school, you would have seen that Saddhu was still going there. But now he was the teacher.

–Rhoda R. Eby

> *"For whosoever shall give you a cup of water to drink in my name ... shall not lose his reward."* –Mark 9:41

Linda Lou's Special Day

Who made Linda Lou's day special?

Linda Lou hopped out of bed and began to dress fast. She must not waste any time. She must find something to do for Jesus.

In Sunday school yesterday the teacher had asked them to do something for Jesus the next day. All the children had **agreed** they would. That was why today was special.

"What do you plan to do?" asked Mother, as Linda Lou put her empty cereal bowl into the sink and turned to go.

"Well, I am not sure," said Linda Lou. "The teacher said if we gave just a cup of cold water to someone, Jesus would be happy, and we would not lose our **reward**.

"I thought I might see a thirsty **hobo** going by on the road. I could give him a cup of cold water.

"Or maybe I could find some old ladies who don't know about Jesus. I could tell them Bible stories.

"Or if I knew a sick woman who lived alone, I could go to her house. I could wash her dishes and sweep for her."

"All those are fine things to do for Jesus," agreed Mother. "But there is no **invalid** that I know of around here. You must think of something else.

"Now before you go, would you please bring the wagon around to the basement door? I need it to take my wash basket to the wash line."

"I am sorry, Mother," said Linda Lou, going out the door. "I do not have time. I must get to work for Jesus. Sammy could do that for you, couldn't he?"

Now where should she begin? No hobo was in sight on the road. All the old ladies she knew went to her church. They all knew more Bible stories than she did. And Mother was right—she could not think of a single invalid who needed her dishes washed or floors swept.

Maybe she would need to go and hunt for someone to help. She started down the front walk.

"Hey, Linda Lou." It was her brother Sammy calling from the shop. "Come here, will you? Hold this board for me a minute."

"I'm sorry, Sammy," she answered. "Our

Sunday school class agreed to do something for Jesus today. I don't have time to help you. Anyway, Mother needs you to take the wagon around to the basement door." Linda Lou opened the yard gate.

Then Mother called from the doorway. "Linda Lou, would you take this jug of ice water out to Daddy? He is fixing fence in the back **pasture**. Or stay here and watch the baby while I go."

"I'm sorry, Mother," Linda Lou called back, as she went out the gate. "I must not waste any time. Let Sammy do that. He is just playing. I told him to get the wagon for you."

She went down the lane to the road. She looked up and down. She saw no hobo on the road who needed a cup of cold water. And, of course, she saw no invalids or old ladies.

At last she thought, *I'll go back the lane to*

the back pasture and ask Daddy. Maybe he can help me plan something special to do for Jesus.

She found Daddy in the back pasture. She watched him hammer nails in the board fence.

"Hi, little gal," he said. "What are you up to?"

Linda Lou sat down in the shade of a tree. "This is my special day. I am out looking for something to do for Jesus, but I can't find anything."

"What kind of thing did you plan to do?" asked Daddy. He laid down his hammer and came over to the shade. He took out a big blue handkerchief and wiped his neck all around inside his shirt collar.

"Well, I thought I might give a cup of cold water to a hobo on the road. Or tell Bible stories to an old lady. Or do the dishes and sweep for some invalid."

"That reminds me," said Daddy. "Mother said she was going to send someone back here with a jug of ice water."

"Oh! Didn't Sammy bring it?" said Linda Lou. "I didn't have time. I had to find something to do for Jesus. We all agreed to, but I can't see anything special to do."

Daddy sat down beside Linda Lou in the grass. "Let me tell you a little story. Then maybe you can think of something to do for Jesus.

"Jesus told how He will come as a King and will give rewards to some people. He will say, 'I am giving you these rewards because you gave Me food and water and clothes when I needed them. You came to see Me when I was sick and when I was in jail.'

"The people will say, 'When did we do all those things for You? We don't remember helping You like that. We were not trying to get any rewards.'

"Then the King will answer, 'When you did those things for someone else because you loved Me, it was the same as doing them for Me.'"

"Then it doesn't matter who you help, just so you do it because you love Jesus. Is that what the story means?"

Daddy nodded. He got up. He picked up his hammer and began to nail another board.

Linda Lou got up too. She must hurry. Of course, it was too late to hold the board for Sammy. It was too late to get the wagon for Mother. But there were lots of other things she could do.

Linda Lou ran down through the pasture to the house. The water jug still sat on the kitchen table.

Ten minutes later Daddy was drinking a cup of cold water. He gave Linda Lou his special smile as he put the lid back on the jug. "I think my little gal is going to have a special day, after all," he said.

"I do too," agreed Linda Lou.

Back at the house all was quiet. Mother was singing in the basement while she did the wash. The baby was in bed for her nap. Sammy was hammering something in the shop.

Very quietly, Linda Lou washed the breakfast dishes. Very quietly she swept the kitchen floor.

Then, as she was putting the broom away, she heard the baby start to fuss. It was not time for her to get up yet. Linda Lou went softly to the crib and picked up her little sister.

She sat in the rocking chair. In a soft

voice she began to tell about the children of Israel going through the **wilderness**.

"They walked, and they walked, and they walked, and they walked."

Linda Lou kept rocking and walking the children of Israel through the wilderness until Baby Sister was fast asleep. Then she laid her softly in her crib and went out on the porch.

"It isn't even dinnertime," she said to herself. "I haven't seen a hobo or an invalid, or any old ladies, but already I have given someone a cup of cold water. I have washed dishes and swept for someone. And I have told someone a Bible story. All that for Jesus. If this is going to be a special day, I guess I am the one who must make it special."

– Ruth K. Hobbs

When Linda Lou really got busy, she did four things for Jesus in a very short time. Sticking with your work and checking off your jobs is a good way to get a lot done. Then you can be free to enjoy your playtime.

Ten Little Duties

Ten little duties! Does no good to whine;
Skip about and do one, then there're only nine.

Nine little duties; it never pays to wait;
Do one quick, and—presto!—there are only eight.

Eight little duties; (might have been eleven);
One done in no time, now there're only seven.

Seven little duties; 'tisn't such a fix;
Do one more, and—just look!—there are only six.

Six little duties; sure as I'm alive!
If you do another one, then there're only five.

4. So he went with them. And when they came to Jordan, they cut down wood.

5. But as one was **felling** a beam, the axe head fell into the water: and he cried, and said, **Alas**, master! for it was **borrowed**.

6. And the man of God said, Where fell it? And he shewed him the place. And he cut down a stick, and cast it in **thither**; and the iron did swim.

7. Therefore said he, Take it up to thee. And he put out his hand, and took it.

– 2 Kings 6:1-7

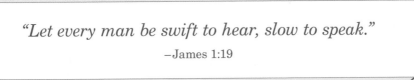

"Let every man be swift to hear, slow to speak."

−James 1:19

I Know, I Know, I Know

What did Ricky know at the end of the story
that he didn't know at the beginning?

Ricky was a busy boy. He was busy with his own thoughts and work and play. He was so busy he did not want to take time to listen to others.

When he sat in church, he listened to the preacher's first few sentences. Then he would say to himself, "I know, I know. I know what he is going to say about that."

Then he would begin thinking about other things. He thought it was not **necessary** to listen to things he already knew.

In Sunday school, he listened to the teacher's first few sentences. Then he would turn his head away and say to himself, "I know, I know. I know that Bible story."

He would look out the window and think about his puppy. Or he would think about what Mother might have for dinner.

At home when Mother began giving him **instructions** for a job, he listened to her first few words. Then he would say, "I know, I know. I know what you want me to do."

Off he would run. He would hurry through the job. Soon he would be back playing.

Often Mother had to call Ricky from his play again. He had not done the job right because he had not listened to all her instructions.

It was a very **ordinary** thing for him to be called back to finish a job. Yet Ricky never **realized** that if he had waited to hear all that Mother wanted to say, it would not be necessary to do a job over again. He never thought about how **rude** it was to run off before others finished speaking. He never realized how rude it was to say, "I know, I know, I know," when someone else was talking.

One morning Ricky was on the way out the back door. He was going to play in his tree house.

He stopped when he saw a dark blue car drive in. He realized it was Aunt Nellie. As soon as she entered the house and saw him she said, "Hello, Ricky. There is a big brown box out in my car . . ."

Before she could say another word, Ricky cried, "I know, I know, I know." It was an ordinary thing for Aunt Nellie to bring him a treat when she came to visit. He could hardly wait to see what it was this time.

Out he ran. In the back seat of Aunt Nellie's car he found the box. There were other boxes too, but this was the only big brown one. This was the one for him.

He took it out. It did not feel very heavy; but he started to the house with it.

Then he stopped. The box really felt empty. He set it down. He pulled open the flaps. The box was empty. It was just an ordinary, empty, brown box.

Now Ricky was really **puzzled**. What were Aunt Nellie's instructions about the big, brown box?

Did she want him to bring the box to the house? Had she started to say why she had brought it? Or was she going to tell him what to do with it? Ricky did not know.

Well, she had started to tell him about the

box. She must have brought it for him to play with. It sure was a nice big box. It would be just the thing for a table in his tree house. That is, if he could get it in the door.

"Sure. That's why she brought it. Now I know," he said to himself.

Ricky was no longer puzzled. He picked up the box and started for the tree house. As he went by the window he stopped and called in, "Thanks a lot, Aunt Nellie. It's just what I needed."

"You're welcome," Aunt Nellie called back. "I thought you'd like that."

It was hard to stuff the brown box through the door of the tree house. But at last it was inside.

For a while he moved things around until he had everything just where it fit the best. He sat on his little stool and looked around. All he needed now was a tablecloth.

Of course, a cloth wasn't necessary. He could use ordinary newspapers, but a cloth would be nicer.

"Mother will have an old sheet or something I can use for a tablecloth," he said to himself.

Ricky went down the ladder. Aunt Nellie had just come out of the house. As she opened her car door, she said in a puzzled voice, "Why, where is my box?"

Ricky looked at her in surprise. "You mean that big brown box?"

Aunt Nellie did not answer. She reached into the car. She took the lid off one of the other boxes that was there.

Then she said, "Ricky, come here. Look at this."

Ricky went and looked. In the box was a dish running over with some brown-and-white-and-pink stuff all mixed up together.

"What is that stuff?" he asked in a puzzled voice.

Aunt Nellie gave a short laugh. But she did not sound as if she thought it were very funny. "That 'stuff' is three dips of ice cream. I picked it up for you at the ice cream store on the way over here. I put the dish in this box and set the big brown box on top so the sun wouldn't shine on it."

"Ice cream," said Ricky in a very small voice. "I didn't know it was there."

"You said, 'I know, I know, I know,' and ran out before I could explain. Then when you called in and thanked me, I thought you had found the ice cream."

"Well—well—I knew you had brought me something. I thought you had brought the big box for my tree house," said Ricky. He looked at that melted ice cream and tried not to think of what he had missed. All that good ice cream gone to waste!

Aunt Nellie lifted the box out of the car. She walked over to a bush and poured out the melted brown-and-white-and-pink stuff.

"What a mess," she said as she watched it drip out of the box.

Then she said, "I have those boxes along because I am going to get apples to can. Now will you please get me some newspapers to put in this messy box? And then . . ."

"I know, I know, I know." The words almost popped out. But Ricky shut his mouth tightly and said nothing. He just stood and listened to the rest of Aunt Nellie's instructions.

". . . please go and get that big brown box. I'll need it for my apples."

Ricky ran to the house and brought some newspapers. He ran to the tree house.

It was harder to get the box out than it had been to get it in. But Ricky was thinking hard the whole time.

He thought about the things his mother had often told him. He thought about how rude it was to run off when others were in the middle of a sentence.

He thought about how rude it was not to listen to the preacher and his teacher while they were talking to him.

He realized now that many times he said, "I know," when he didn't really know at all— like he had done today.

"I'm not going to say that anymore," he told himself as he backed down the ladder with the big brown box. "Who wants to be rude? If I listen until people are finished talking, I just might save myself a lot of trouble. After today, that's something I really *do* know."

– Eileen M. Hasse

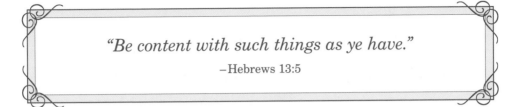

> *"Be content with such things as ye have."*
>
> —Hebrews 13:5

Worse Than a Patch

What do you think Judy whispered to herself?

It was Saturday before the first day of school. Judy and Mother drove to the part of town where the big stores were. Mother parked the car and they walked toward one of the big stores.

"Mother, will you get me a new bag for my schoolbooks? That one of Bobby's that I used last year is so ugly and patched. I **despise** patches. They're so ugly," said Judy.

"Well, Judy, I know that bag did not **satisfy** you, but a schoolbag can carry books even when it is ugly and patched," said Mother. "Those patches kept your books from falling out, didn't they? We can't spend money for things just for pretty."

Then Mother smiled. "But I did plan to get you a new bag today. That old one of Bobby's is worn out. I can't patch it anymore."

"Oh, goody, goody, goody," sang Judy, as they went into the store. "May I go and **select** the one I want?"

"Yes, you may. And when you find one that satisfies you, bring it to the checkout, and wait for me," said Mother.

Judy hurried to the back of the store where the school things were. And there stood her best friend, Millie, who lived next door.

"Why, Millie, I didn't know you were coming to town today. What are you getting?"

"A new schoolbag. Mama said I could select the one I want. She's over there getting some yarn for Grandma."

"I came for a schoolbag too. That old patched one of Bobby's is worn out. And I'm glad! I despise patched things. Did you pick yours yet?"

"No," replied Millie. "There are so many colors, I can't **decide**. Which do you like?"

Judy looked at the pile of schoolbags. "Well, I don't like that orange-and-black one. And I don't like this purple-and-pink one. But this light-and-dark-blue one is pretty. I would like this one."

"I think that one is pretty too," said Millie. "That's the one I was looking at. Let's get them alike."

"Yes, let's! We'll have to put our names on them or we'll get them mixed up at school. I can hardly wait till Monday!"

"Neither can I. After supper this evening, let's take our bags down the street and show them to Sue and Tessie."

"All right. I wonder if they will decide to get new ones too."

Each of the girls selected a light-and-dark-blue bag. Millie went to find her mother and Judy went to the front of the store.

After supper the two girls met on the sidewalk. Both had their new schoolbags.

"What do you have in yours?" asked Judy the minute she saw Millie.

"It's the yarn Mama got for Grandma. I must stop and drop it off at her house as we go by."

When they got to the house where Millie's

grandma lived, Millie said, "I'll just take the yarn and run in, unless you want to go in too."

"No, I'll sit here and wait for you."

"Grandma will want to talk, but I'll try to hurry." Millie took the yarn from her bag and laid the bag on the grass beside Judy. She ran up the walk to the house.

While she waited, Judy played with her bag. Suddenly she saw something. On the bottom, right along the seam, was a long, six-inch slit. It was so close to the seam it was hard to see. But Judy knew if she put anything into the bag it would fall right out.

"Oh, my bag is no good! No good at all!" she whispered. "We'll have to go back and get another one." Even as she said it, she knew that Mother would not make another trip back to the store just for another schoolbag.

"She'll try to fix it. She'll take some blue cloth and put a patch on it. I know she will! Then I'll have another patched schoolbag!"

Judy sat and let the tears come. Then she wiped them away. "It's not fair!" she said crossly to herself. "I carried a patched schoolbag all last year. I shouldn't have to carry one this year! I despise patches!

"Why did I have to get this one? Why didn't Millie select it? She could have picked it just as easily as I did!"

She looked at Millie's bag on the grass beside her. She picked it up. She looked toward the house. Millie was not coming yet.

Judy laid both bags in her lap. She put hers on top. Then she put Millie's on top. Then hers. Then Millie's. She did this again and again until she wasn't really sure which was which.

"I'll put one of them on the grass. That

will be Millie's," she decided. "I can say I got them mixed up and didn't know which was which. I can say it doesn't matter because both are alike. That should satisfy her if she asks."

But when Judy laid one of the bags on the grass beside her, she did know which one it was.

Millie was gone a long time. Judy didn't mind waiting for her. Somehow she did not want to face her friend.

Every time she looked at the bag in her lap, she thought, *I stole Millie's bag.*

Every time she looked at the bag on the grass she said out loud, "It isn't fair for me to have a patched bag this year. I had one last year!" Then the tears would come again.

At last Millie came running from the house.

"Oh, Judy. I'm sorry I was gone so long.

Grandma just talked and talked and talked! I couldn't get away!"

"That's all right," said Judy, getting up. "I don't care. It's so late now. Let's go on home."

"All right," said Millie, picking up the bag from the grass. "Tessie and Sue don't have to see our bags today. They will see them at school on Monday."

At home, Judy tried to act happy over her new schoolbag. Mother thought it was pretty and so did Daddy.

Bobby said, "It was time you got a new bag. Mother won't have to patch this one for a long time. All the fussing you did last year over my old bag, I know there is nothing in the world you despise more than a patch."

Judy knew Bobby was teasing her, but she couldn't even smile. She just said, "I'm going back to my room and put all my school things in it. Then I'll be ready for school on Monday morning."

Judy went to her room, but she did not put anything into the bag. She went to the window and looked over at Millie's house. "I wonder what she is doing," she said to herself. "I wonder if she is putting her school things into her bag. I wonder if she saw that slit along the seam yet."

Suddenly she whispered something to herself. Then she went out to the kitchen. "Mother, may I run over to Millie's a minute? I need to tell her something."

"Why, Judy, you were with Millie only fifteen minutes ago. And why are you taking your new schoolbag along? Is this something that must be said tonight?"

"Yes, Mother, I must tell her tonight. I really must. I can't be satisfied unless I do. It is something I just found out."

"Just found out! What did you find out in fifteen minutes?"

"I just found out that some things are worse than a patch. I'll tell you about it when I get back."

–Author Unknown

This poem tells of something Judy and Millie might have heard that last Saturday before school began if they had lived in the country.

Autumn

The katydid says it
    as plain as can be;
And the crickets are singing it
    under the tree;

In the aster's blue eyes
    you may read
      the same hint,
       Just as clearly
        as if you had seen it
         in print;

And the corn sighs it too,
as it waves in the sun;
That autumn is here, and summer is done.

–Persis Gardiner

122

Fall days at the beginning of school are a good time to watch for all kinds of seeds and the different ways God planned for them to be scattered for next year's plants.

Baby Seeds

In a milkweed cradle,
Snug and warm,
Baby seeds are hiding,
Safe from harm.

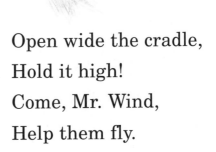

Open wide the cradle,
Hold it high!
Come, Mr. Wind,
Help them fly.

—*Author Unknown*

123

"For ye have need of patience."

−Hebrews 10:36

Sticking With It

Who was to blame for the trouble with
fractions, Skippy, and the woodpile?

Fred balled up his paper. He threw it into the trash can. "Mama, I can't do this math. It's **fractions**. I used up a whole sheet of paper, and I still can't do it. Fractions are just impossible."

"When did you start learning fractions?" asked Mama, putting down her book.

"On Monday."

"This is only Wednesday. No wonder fractions seem hard. You have not worked at them long enough. Fractions are not impossible."

"I tried in school, and I tried now. I still can't do them," said Fred with a glum look. "Fractions are too hard, anyway. I'm not smart enough to do them."

"You can't learn something new by trying just two times," said Mama. "Show me your math lesson. I will help you. Boys your age have learned fractions for hundreds of years. There's no trick to fractions. They are not impossible at all. You just have not put your mind to it. You have not stuck with it long enough. Be **patient** and keep trying."

"But I can't understand them. The teacher said we must remember that the bigger the bottom number is, the less it is. That does not make any **sense**."

"Oh, yes, it does," said Mama. She sat down beside Fred at the table. "The teacher was right. Let me show you."

Mama went over the lesson with Fred. After a while it was finished.

"Thank you, Mama. At least I have this page done. But I know I won't be able to do them by myself in school tomorrow."

"I think you could have done this lesson by yourself if you had put your mind to it. At least you should have tried a little longer," said Mama, going back to her book. "You didn't give yourself a chance to learn them."

A few days later, Fred was in the back yard with Skippy. He was trying to teach the little dog to shake hands.

Before long he came into the house. "Mama, do you think Skippy is as smart as Mark Miller's dog?"

"Yes, I think so," answered Mama. "Most

dogs are pretty smart."

"Well, Mark's dog can shake hands as nice as you please when you say, 'Shake,' but Skippy just jumps up on me. He can't seem to catch on. I don't think he is very smart."

"How long have you been trying to teach Skippy?" asked Mama.

"I started yesterday after school. Then I tried again today. But he acts as if he doesn't know what it's all about."

Mama laughed. "No wonder, Fred. Skippy doesn't know what it's all about. Shaking hands doesn't make any sense to dogs. It's just a trick people like to teach them. Don't blame Skippy. Ever since I was a little girl, I've known dogs that could shake hands. Be patient with Skippy. He'll catch on. Shaking hands is an easy trick for a dog to learn."

The very next day, Fred was given the job

of stacking the pile of wood that his father had split. He worked ten minutes. Then the whole stack fell down.

Fred came in with a glum look on his face. "It's impossible to stack that old wood. It just won't stay up."

"Did you do it like Father showed you?"

"Well, I don't remember just how he said to do it. But how can there be a right way and a wrong way to stack wood?"

"There must be a wrong way, or your stack would not have fallen down," said Mama.

"But, Mama, the wood is all shapes and sizes. There is no sense in trying to make that kind of wood stay on a nice stack."

"There is a trick to it," said Mama. "But don't blame the wood, Fred. Everyone else around here has wood in nice stacks. Did you put your mind to the job? Did you try to see what you were doing wrong?"

"No."

"You can't learn to stack wood in ten minutes. You must think about what you are doing and stick with it."

"All right," said Fred. "When Father comes home, I'll ask him to show me again how to do it. At least I tried."

Then Fred took a small bag from his pocket. He untied the strings. "Watch how good I am at jacks now, Mama," he said.

He **poured** the jacks out on the table. Then he tossed up the little ball and began. He went up to the "fives" before he missed.

"Why, Fred," said Mama, much surprised. "I didn't know you were that good. The last time I watched, you couldn't even do the 'ones.' And that was not very long ago."

"I know," said Fred, smiling happily.

"But now I'm good enough that the big boys let me play with them at school."

"How did you catch on so soon?" asked Mama.

"Well, I really wanted to learn how, so I kept my jacks in my pocket. Every chance I got, I played by myself. I made myself start at the 'ones' every time and kept **pegging** away at it. And the next thing I knew I could do it."

"Seems like there was a boy around here not so long ago who said he could never get past the 'ones.' I think I heard him say learning to play jacks was impossible—that he was not smart enough, and there wasn't any sense to the game anyway."

At Mama's words, Fred got a little red in the face. But he laughed and said, "Well, Mama, this is a game you must put your mind to. There's a trick to it. You must learn how to pour out the jacks just right. Then before you toss up the ball, you must plan which ones you are going to grab. And you must toss the ball up just right too.

"If you do it over and over and keep working at it, soon it gets easy. It didn't take me long when I stuck with it."

"I see," said Mama. "Do you think putting your mind to it and sticking with it would work with other things?"

"Oh, yes, I think it would," said Fred.

"You mean like doing fractions and teaching Skippy and stacking wood?" asked Mama.

Fred looked at Mama in surprise for a minute. Then he began picking up his jacks. He put them in the bag. He put the bag in his pocket. He smiled at Mama. "I guess I'll go and try it on that woodpile," he said.

–Author Unknown

*Find a line in this poem and in the next that shows
that each dog's owner likes him just the way he is.*

The Hairy Dog

My dog's so furry
    I've not seen
His face for years
    and years;
His eyes are buried
    out of sight,
I only guess his ears.

When people ask me
    for his breed,
I do not know or care:
He has the beauty
    of them all
Hidden beneath
    his hair.

    – Herbert Asquith

My Dog

His nose is short and scrubby;
   His ears hang rather low;
And he always brings the stick back,
   No matter how far you throw.

He gets spanked rather often
   For things he shouldn't do,
Like lying on beds, and barking,
   And eating up shoes when they're new.

He always wants to be going
   Where he isn't supposed to go.
He tracks up the house when it's snowing—
   Oh, puppy, I love you so.

                    —Marchette Chute

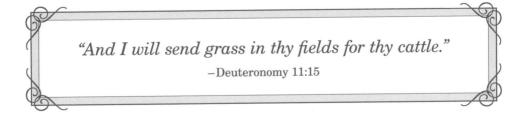

"And I will send grass in thy fields for thy cattle."

–Deuteronomy 11:15

Cow With a Secret

What is the difference in the way cows were cared for in Switzerland and the way they are cared for in our country?

Irmgard was a little **Swiss** girl. She lived in **Switzerland**.

She had a cow. Yes, a cow of her very own. Her uncle had given it to her. He lived far away across the Swiss mountains.

He had sent the cow with her brother Peter. He had sent a **message** which pleased Irmgard very much.

"Tell Irmgard that this cow is her own. Her name is Forget-Me-Not. That is the name of a flower that grows on the high mountains. Irmgard must learn to milk and make butter. I will come at Christmas to see her. I shall want some butter made by her own hands. The butter will be my Christmas gift.

"And tell her the cow has a secret."

You can imagine how Irmgard felt when she heard this. Her sister Rose said, "I cannot tell you what the secret is, but I will teach you how to do all those things as soon as the cows come home from their summer pasture. And you will know the secret the instant Forget-Me-Not comes home."

"How can a cow have a secret? How can a cow tell anything?" asked Irmgard. She asked her mother and father. She asked Rose and Peter. But they just smiled.

"Wait and see," they said. "Forget-Me-Not will tell you when she gets back from the mountain pasture in the fall."

Every spring in Switzerland, the men and boys take the village cows to pastures high up in the **Alps**. Every family sends its cows to where the grass grows fresh and green and the cool winds blow all summer long.

The older girls go too. They take care of the milk. They make cheese from the milk. They all work happily in the mountain pastures till snow comes in the fall.

Irmgard wanted her cow to go with the others from the village. She told Forget-Me-Not all about the fresh green grass high up on the mountains.

"The cows will be going to pasture very soon," she said. "I know you would like to go too, so I shall let you. I shall let you go where the forget-me-nots bloom and the grass grows green. Brother Peter says that it is a most wonderful place. You can see the snow on the top of the mountain while you eat the grass.

"You must grow fat, you know, and give a great deal of milk. When you come back in the fall, I shall milk you myself. And I shall make butter and cheese. And you must tell me the secret the **instant** you get back."

It was a great day when the cows started to the pasture. All the cows in the village went. They wore bells around their necks.

The lead cow wore the biggest bell. The instant she started up the path the cows of each family fell into line behind her.

Tinkle, tinkle, tinkle, went the bells as the cows started up the mountain path one after the other.

Irmgard's cow had ribbons on her horns.

"Mine is the prettiest cow in the whole line," said the little girl.

"Good-bye," said her brother Peter.

"Good-bye," said her sister Rose.

"Good-bye," cried Irmgard. "Good-bye, Forget-Me-Not. Hurry back and tell me the secret the very instant you get home."

Irmgard watched the cows going up the mountain path as long as she could see them. Once her cow looked back and called, "Moo, moo!" just as if she were sending a last message back to the girl, "I'll do what you said."

Then up the mountain path went the cows. Up the path went the men and boys and the older girls.

————⊰✿⊱————

Summer was a busy time for Irmgard. She was her mother's only helper when Rose was away. There was always so much for her to do that she sometimes forgot to think about the secret.

The days slipped by quickly. Irmgard was surprised one evening in the early fall when her father said, "I saw the cows far up the mountain coming down the path today. They will be here tomorrow."

"Tomorrow!" cried Irmgard in great excitement.

"Yes, tomorrow," said her father, "and your cow—" He stopped. He put his hand over his mouth.

"I can't tell. It is a secret," he said.

"Oh, Father, Father, please tell!" she begged. "What is it about Forget-Me-Not? Did someone send you a message about her?"

But her father would not tell. "I can't tell, even if you guess it," he said. "Peter and Rose said to me again and again, before they left,

'Don't tell Irmgard that her cow ...'"

Irmgard could not keep from trying to guess. "Forget-Me-Not gives more milk than any other cow."

No, that was not right; she knew by her father's smile.

"Her milk is the richest. Her butter and cheese are the best?"

Still she was wrong.

"Oh, Mother!" she cried, "What do you think it can be?"

"I am not going to guess," said her mother, "because it is a secret. Maybe you will dream it when you go to sleep tonight. Anyway, you will know the instant Forget-Me-Not comes in the morning."

So Irmgard went to sleep. She dreamed all night of cool pastures and fresh green grass and pretty cows with ribbons on their horns. But she did not dream about the secret.

Early the next morning Irmgard went out and sat by the roadside. She waited and watched—waited and watched. She thought she could not wait another minute.

Just then she heard a sound far up the path. *Tinkle, tinkle!* it said.

Irmgard knew what that meant.

The cows were coming! *Tinkle, tinkle!* They were a little nearer. *Tinkle, tinkle!* Now she could see them.

First came the leader. She wore her big bell. Then came the other cows. They were sleek and fat.

The first men nodded to the little girl. "Good morning, Irmgard," they said. They smiled as if they knew the secret.

Then came her neighbor with his cows. He, too, looked at Irmgard and called out as he passed, "Good news for you, Irmgard."

"Oh, what can it be? What can it be?" cried Irmgard. "Will our cows never come?"

At last their cows came slowly down the path. There were six of them.

"We know," they seemed to say, "but we cannot tell."

Irmgard almost held her breath with excitement. There came her sister Rose. She was smiling. There came her brother Peter. He was smiling too. And there came Forget-Me-Not—and close behind trotted the dearest, loveliest, frisky baby calf!

The secret was out. Irmgard was the happiest little girl in Switzerland. Her cow had a calf!

– Maud Lindsay

Here is a poem that could fit Irmgard's cow and calf.

The New Baby Calf

Buttercup, the cow, had a new baby calf,
    A fine baby calf,
    A strong baby calf,
Not strong like his mother
But strong for a calf,
    For this baby calf was so new!

Buttercup licked him with her strong
    warm tongue,
Buttercup washed him with her strong
    warm tongue,
Buttercup brushed him with her strong
    warm tongue,
    And the baby calf liked that!

The new baby calf took a very little walk,
　　A tiny little walk,
　　A teeny little walk,
But his long legs wobbled
When he took a little walk,
　　And the new baby calf fell down.

Buttercup told him with a low soft *Moo-oo*
That he was doing very well for one
　　so very new.
And she talked very gently,
　　as mother cows do,
　　　And the new baby calf liked that!

The new baby calf took another little walk,
　　A little longer walk,
　　A little stronger walk,
He walked around his mother
And he found the place to drink,
　　And the new baby calf liked that!

Buttercup told him with another low moo
That drinking milk from Mother
    was a fine thing to do,
That she had lots of milk for him
    and for the farmer too,
      And the baby calf liked that!

The new baby calf drank milk every day,
His legs grew so strong
    that he could run and play,
He learned to eat grass and then grain and hay,
    And the big baby calf grew fat!

—*Edith H. Newlin*

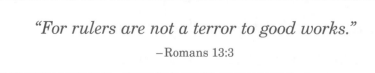

> *"For rulers are not a terror to good works."*
>
> —Romans 13:3

Here Comes the Principal

Part 1

Did Ronnie have a real reason to fear the principal in this part of the story?

Ronnie and his friend Ted liked second grade. They liked it better than first grade, **except** for one thing. They were afraid of the new **principal**. At least Ronnie was.

Last year's principal was short. He looked old. He walked as if he were tired all the time. He never went out and played with the students. But he was jolly. He smiled when he met you in the hall.

Mr. Dickon was not short. He was big and tall. Mr. Dickon was not old and tired. He was young. He walked with long, fast steps. He went out and played with the upper grade boys, but he was not jolly. The boys had not seen him smile one time yet.

One day Ronnie and Ted were sitting on the school bus behind two upper-grade boys.

One boy said to the other, "So you had to go to the principal's **office**! What did he do to you?"

"Never mind," said the other, with a short laugh. "Mr. Dickon is all right, but I hope I never have to go to his office again. I'm going to **dodge** him after this. Watch what you do, or he'll call you in too."

"I will watch myself," said the first boy.

"It looks as if he's going to make us walk the chalk line this year!"

When Ted and Ronnie got off the bus they looked at each other.

"What does 'walk the chalk line' mean?" asked Ronnie.

"I don't know," answered Ted. "It is something those upper-grade boys don't want to do."

"You can tell they are afraid of the new principal too," said Ronnie. "We had better watch out. I sure don't want to go to his office!"

At the supper table that evening, Ronnie asked, "Daddy, what does it mean to 'walk the chalk line'?"

"It means you must be careful to do what you are supposed to do."

"Is that all?"

"Yes, that is all. Why do you ask?"

"I heard some of the upper-grade boys saying the new principal is going to make them 'walk the chalk line' this year. They sounded as if they were afraid of the new principal. They said they sure were going to dodge him."

Daddy laughed. "That's good. Some of those upper-grade boys need to be afraid of the principal. They need to walk the chalk line.

"But, Ronnie, you don't need to **worry** about that except when you disobey. Do what you are supposed to do, and you will not need to be afraid of the principal."

Ronnie said no more. But he thought, *I do need to worry. I am afraid of Mr. Dickon. He is so big, and he never smiles. How can I tell if I'm walking his chalk line or not? I'd better just dodge him if I can.*

The next morning on the bus, Ronnie told Ted what Daddy had said.

"Well then," said Ted, "we don't need to worry except when we do something wrong."

"Maybe not," said Ronnie, "but I'm going to stay out of his way. How will we know when he might want to take us to his office?"

Just then the bus stopped at the school building. The driver opened the door. All the children stood.

Suddenly Ronnie grabbed Ted's arm and whispered, "Here comes the principal!"

Both boys sat down again. Ronnie dodged behind some of the other children.

Mr. Dickon came up the steps of the school bus. "Good morning, everyone. I just came to tell you that the bus will not be left at school today. It's going to the shop to get fixed. Just be sure you take your books and everything with you."

"I won't forget my crutches," piped up Justin from the front seat. Justin was in the first grade. He had a broken leg. His leg was in a cast. He always sat in the front seat so he could get off first.

Mr. Dickon stepped down on the sidewalk. He lifted Justin down, cast, crutches, and all. Then, carrying the little boy's lunch box and book, he walked beside him to the school building. He held the door open till Justin swung in on his crutches.

Ronnie and Ted had waited. They wanted to be the last ones in. "That was nice of him," said Ted. "I saw him smiling at Justin."

"Well, I didn't," said Ronnie. "I'm still going to stay as far away from him as I can."

That morning on the playground, the second-graders wanted to play dodgeball. Miss Neff said, "Ronnie and Ted, will you run to the building and get us two good balls, please?"

Away went the boys. They pulled open the big doors. They ran for the hall closet where the balls and bats were kept. Just as they got there, someone called, "Boys! No running in the building!" It was the principal, coming down the hall with long, fast steps.

– Ruth K. Hobbs

> "Wilt thou then not be afraid of the power?
> Do that which is good." –Romans 13:3

Here Comes the Principal

Part 2

*Did Ronnie have a real reason to fear the
principal in this part of the story?*

Ronnie and Ted dodged into the closet.
They turned on the light. They pulled the
door partway shut. They took a long time
picking out the balls they wanted. Any
minute they were sure the principal would

put his head in the door. But he didn't.

At last Ronnie whispered, "Is he still out there?"

Ted peeped through the crack of the half-open door. "I don't see him," he whispered back.

Then the boys turned out the closet light. They looked out. No one was in sight except an upper-grade boy sweeping the hall.

As they came by, he said, "You little boys had better watch out! If you ever have to go to the principal's office, you'll be sorry!"

Ronnie and Ted looked at the big boy, but they did not say anything. They walked quietly down the hall and out the door.

Outside, Ronnie asked, "What do you think Mr. Dickon would do to us if he took us to his office for running in the building?"

"I don't know," said Ted. "But it's like

your dad said; if we do what we are supposed to do, we don't need to be afraid. It would be our fault if he called us in. We ran in the building. We know we are not supposed to do that. We just better walk the chalk line so we don't need to be afraid of him."

"Well, it's hard to remember everything all the time," said Ronnie.

At noon that day, Ted and Ronnie sat on the grass and watched the upper-grade boys playing softball. The inning was over. One team was coming in to bat. The other team was going out to the field.

Suddenly Ronnie jumped up. He whispered, "Here comes the principal! Let's go!"

"Why?" asked Ted. "He's not going to do anything to us."

"How do you know? He might be coming to get us for running in the building."

"Aw, no," said Ted. "He would have come to the closet when we were in there, if that's what he wanted."

"Well, I'm afraid of him. I don't want to go to his office. We can run to the other side of the field and watch the game from there. Come on, Ted!"

"Miss Neff said we should not cross the field when they are playing," said Ted.

"They aren't really playing now. They are just changing sides. Come on!"

"No. Look, Ronnie, they are throwing the ball back and forth, and Miss Neff said ..."

But Ronnie was gone. He was dodging between the boys who were coming in to bat, and those going out to the field.

Suddenly he heard two boys shout at the same time, "Watch it, Ronnie! Look out for Ronnie!"

Then he felt a blow on the back of his head. It felt as though someone had hit him with a hammer! Down he went. A thousand stars spun around and around in his head.

When he opened his eyes he saw scared, white faces looking down at him. Just before darkness came over him, Ronnie heard another shout, "Get back! Here comes the principal!"

When Ronnie came to again, someone was carrying him. Someone was saying his name quietly over and over, "Ronnie? Ronnie? Ronnie? Can you hear me?"

He opened his eyes and looked into the face of Mr. Dickon. He tried to sit up, but the principal held him gently. He smiled and said, "I've got you, Ronnie. Don't worry. You are going to be all right."

"What happened to me?" whispered Ronnie. "My head! It hurts!"

"I'm sure it does!" said Mr. Dickon. And he smiled a bigger smile. "A ball hit you. But you'll be all right pretty soon.

"I'm taking you to my office where you can lie down till you feel better."

To the principal's office!

Ronnie opened his eyes wide! He looked for one long minute into the eyes above him. And suddenly he wasn't afraid anymore. And he knew why.

Now they were in the building. Someone held open the door to the principal's office.

Mr. Dickon carried him in and laid him on a sofa.

Pain began to beat in Ronnie's head, but he looked up at the principal and said, "I'm sorry I ran across the field. It was my fault. Miss Neff told us not to. I'm going to walk the chalk line after this. You'll see."

– Ruth K. Hobbs

Message From the Sky

How would the shepherds know which of the babies in Bethlehem was the Saviour?

8. And there were in the same country shepherds **abiding** in the field, keeping watch over their flock by night.

9. And, lo, the angel of the Lord came upon them, and the glory of the Lord shone round about them: and they were sore afraid.

10. And the angel said unto them, Fear not: for, behold, I bring you good **tidings** of great joy, which shall be to all people.

11. For unto you is born this day
    in the city of David a Saviour,
    which is Christ the Lord.

12. And this shall be a sign unto you;
    Ye shall find the babe wrapped in
    swaddling clothes, lying in a **manger.**

13. And suddenly there was with the angel a
    multitude of the **heavenly host** praising God,
    and saying,

14. Glory to God in the highest, and on earth
    peace, good will toward men.

15. And it came to pass, as the angels were gone
    away from them into heaven, the shepherds
    said one to another, Let us now go even unto
    Bethlehem, and see this thing which is come
    to pass, which the Lord hath made known
    unto us.

16. And they came with **haste,** and found Mary,
    and Joseph, and the babe lying in a manger.

17. And when they had seen it, they made known abroad the saying which was told them **concerning** this child.

18. And all they that heard it wondered at those things which were told them by the shepherds.

19. But Mary kept all these things, and **pondered** them in her heart.

20. And the shepherds returned, **glorifying** and praising God for all the things that they had heard and seen, as it was told unto them.

– Luke 2:8-20

> *"Thou shalt not be afraid for the terror by night."*
>
> —Psalm 91:5

Whom Shall I Fear?

A Story From Africa

Would you have done what Wembo did?

"**Wembo**," called Mama from the little hut. "Will you please run to the missionary's house before it gets dark? Ask how **Lusa** is getting along. Her leg looked so bad this morning when I took her there. It was all **swollen** from that spider bite. Sister **Manning** thought she had **medicine** that would make the leg better."

"Yes, Mama," answered Wembo. "It won't take me long."

Wembo washed his hands and face. He put on a clean shirt. He had been thinking of his little sister all afternoon. Her swollen leg had looked **terrible** to him. He would be glad to find out how she was.

It was kind of Sister Manning to take care of Lusa at the missionary's house.

There was a hospital on the other side of the **jungle**. But you do not usually go to the hospital for a spider bite.

"You should be back before the sun goes down," said Mama. "Anyway, remember that Jesus is the Light of the world. He will go with you."

"I know, Mama," said Wembo. "My last Bible verse was 'I will never leave you.' I will say that verse and run fast. It will not take me an hour. You will see me before dark."

Off he ran down the hot **African** path that led over the hill to the missionary's house.

Sister Manning came to the door. "Oh, Wembo," she cried when she saw him. "I am so glad you came. I was praying that God would send someone. Your little sister needs medicine that I do not have here. Her leg looks terrible. You must go to the hospital and get it!"

"Me?" asked Wembo. The road to the hospital led through the jungle.

"Yes, you. There is no one else to go. The other missionaries will not come back until late tonight. You can ride my bicycle."

Wembo looked at the red bicycle by the porch. He loved to ride it!

But then he looked at the jungle. The sun shone like a red eye through the black trees. It would be out of sight before he got to the hospital. It would be black night before he got back.

Of course, the red bicycle had a headlight. But Wembo thought of the stories told by the witch doctor. He was thinking of the terrible things the **witch doctor** said walked in the jungle at night. Wembo had heard those stories since he was a little boy.

Wembo knew about God and Jesus. He did not believe those scary stories. But he could not forget them. That was why he did not go outside his hut at night by himself, if he could help it.

"Here, take this paper," Sister Manning said. "Give it to the doctor. He will know what kind of medicine to send.

"And hurry. Lusa has been crying all afternoon. She should have had the medicine hours ago. But there was no one to send."

"Sister Manning," said Wembo. "It will

be dark . . ." He stopped.

"I know. But the bicycle headlight is bright. You will be able to see the road just fine."

Wembo took the paper and put it into his pocket. But still he stood there.

Then the missionary said, "Wembo, are you thinking of the terrible stories the witch doctor tells? You know they are not true."

"I know. But I have never been in the jungle after dark all by myself."

"But you will not be alone, Wembo. Jesus will go with you. He will take care of you."

"That is what Mama said. I guess I was not thinking of my verse, 'I will never leave you.'"

Wembo stood there for only a minute. And in that minute he could hear Lusa crying. Then he said, "I will go. I will say that verse as I ride through the jungle."

"I will give you another verse to say," said Sister Manning. " 'The Lord is my light and my salvation. Whom shall I fear?' "

"Remember, Wembo, Jesus is the Light of the world. Darkness is nothing to Him. I will be praying for you. Now you must go!"

"Thank you," said Wembo, as he got on the bicycle. "I am going to say those verses all the way. 'I will never leave you,' 'The Lord is my light,' and 'Whom shall I fear?' "

Off he rode as fast as he could. He had not gone far when he saw the last of the red sun slide down behind the trees.

When he rode into the jungle it was almost dark. He turned on the bicycle headlight. It made a friendly bright circle on the dust of the road.

"I will never leave you.

"The Lord is my light.

"Whom shall I fear?"

He whispered the verses to himself as he rode deeper and deeper into the jungle.

Wembo put the stories of the witch doctor out of his mind. He thought of his home. Mama would be cooking supper over a bright fire. She would wonder why he had not come home. He had been gone more than an hour already.

He thought of the missionary's house with its lighted rooms. He wished he were there right now. It wouldn't take him long to go back.

But then he thought of Lusa. She had cried all afternoon. That made him ride faster. He began to whisper the verses to himself again:

"I will never leave you.

"The Lord is my light.

"Whom shall I fear?"

Wembo came out of the jungle. He saw the lights of the little town. He saw the lights of the hospital.

A few more minutes and he was safe inside. He gave the paper to the doctor. He told him about Lusa's leg and how she had been crying all afternoon.

The doctor went to get the medicine. Wembo sat down to rest. How tired he was! He had not felt tired while he was riding. But now he wished he could curl up and go to sleep.

When the doctor came back he said, "I am giving you two kinds of medicine. One is for your sister's leg. The other is to take away the pain and help her to sleep."

Then he asked, "Did you come alone?"

"No," said Wembo. "Jesus came with me. And He is going back with me too."

The doctor just looked at him.

"I was really pretty scared, but I said my verses, and that helped."

"What verses?" asked the doctor.

Wembo said his verses again:

" 'I will never leave you.' "

" 'The Lord is my light.' "

" 'Whom shall I fear?' "

"You need a light in that jungle, all right," said the doctor. "And you need someone to be with you too. The jungle is not the best place to be after dark. But you are a brave boy. I hope your little sister will get well soon."

There was no light in the sky at all when Wembo left the hospital. Nothing but the stars. When he left the open path and rode into the jungle, he could not see even the stars.

In all his life, Wembo had never been alone in such black darkness! The white circle of the headlight was all he could see.

But he could hear all kinds of things. Night birds called. Frogs croaked. Leaves rustled. Insects sang. Branches cracked. Grass swished. And Wembo could only guess what animals made the other sounds he heard.

"'I will never leave you.'" Wembo said it out loud.

"'The Lord is my light.'" He said this louder yet.

Then, just ahead of him, the bicycle light picked up two yellow eyes in the middle of the road. Two yellow eyes like two yellow lights.

Wembo put on the brakes for just a moment. Then he shouted at the top of his voice, "'Whom shall I fear?'" He rode at the yellow eyes as hard as he could.

The eyes went out. Something crashed away through the bushes.

Wembo rode on. But now he was hardly scared at all. His verses had become almost a song. He sang them out loud as he rode:

"'I will never leave you.'

"'The Lord is my light.'

"'Whom shall I fear?'"

It didn't seem long at all before Wembo came out of the jungle. Now he was on the open path. Now he could see the friendly lights of the missionary's house.

He had made it! Jesus really had gone with him!

"'I will never leave you,'" he said, as he got off the bicycle and felt for the medicine in his pocket.

"'The Lord is my light,'" he said, as he

went up the steps.

And as he crossed the porch, he was saying, "'Whom shall I fear?'"

Wembo opened the door. "No one," he said as he went in.

– Esther Miller Payler

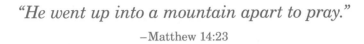

"He went up into a mountain apart to pray."

—Matthew 14:23

Mrs. Cut-Cut's Close Call

Why didn't the children cry and beg their parents not to kill Mrs. Cut-Cut?

"I think that old white hen must go," said Mother. "The children have not brought in any white eggs for days and days."

"She looks so nice and fat," said Daddy. "I thought she was a good **layer**. But I guess she is too old to lay. We cannot feed a hen that does not lay eggs."

"Fat hens make the best chicken potpie," said Mother. "Wouldn't that be good for Sunday dinner?"

"Yes, it would," answered Daddy. "Just tell me when you want me to cut off her head."

Fay and Jerry heard what Mother and Daddy said. They looked at each other. Then they went out of the house. They went to the woodpile near the henhouse. They sat on the wood and looked at the hens.

Red hens were going in and out of the henhouse. Red hens were **scratching** in the dirt. Red hens were under the blackberry bushes looking for bugs. Red hens were in the barnyard scratching around the straw bales.

All the hens were red except one. That was

Mrs. Cut-Cut. She was all white with yellow legs. She was scratching by the woodpile.

She looked at Fay and Jerry as they came up. "Cut-cut-cut-ca-dah-ca," she **cackled**, as if to say, "Hello, Fay and Jerry, isn't this a nice day?"

"They mustn't kill Mrs. Cut-Cut," said Jerry. "She is our pet."

"Mother and Daddy do not know she is our pet," said Fay.

"But hens must lay eggs. Layers are no good if they don't lay eggs," said Jerry.

"I couldn't eat a bit of chicken potpie if it were made out of Mrs. Cut-Cut," said Fay.

"But what can we do? The red hens lay brown eggs. Mrs. Cut-Cut lays white eggs. We have not found any white eggs for days and days. So Mother knows Mrs. Cut-Cut is not laying."

"Daddy said she looks like a good layer," cried Fay.

"I know," said Jerry, "but she is not laying."

"I don't think she eats much chicken feed," said Fay.

"Maybe she doesn't now. But as soon as it gets cold, Daddy will shut them in the hen-house. Then chicken feed is all she will eat."

"Cut-cut-cut-ca-dah-ca," cackled Mrs. Cut-Cut, as if to say, "That will be all right with me." Then she went on scratching.

"Do you think this is important enough to tell God about?" asked Jerry. "Should we ask Him to save Mrs. Cut-Cut?"

"It would not be a selfish prayer," said Fay. "We would be saving her life. If God sees when a **sparrow** falls, He would see when Daddy cut off Mrs. Cut-Cut's head."

"That's right. Let's go up to the Lookout

and ask God to save Mrs. Cut-Cut's life," said Jerry.

The children went up into the hay barn. They went to the big open door. From there they could look out over the farm. That is why they called that place the Lookout.

From there they could see across the pasture to the green line of trees where the creek ran.

They could see the white house with its red roof. They could see the yard and the wash on the clothesline.

They could see the brown woodpile. They could see the row of round hay bales covered with white plastic. They could see the garden and the blackberry bushes. They could look down on the henhouse and the barnyard.

The Lookout was a wonderful place to sit and talk and look out over the world. It was a good place to talk with God.

Fay and Jerry both prayed. They asked God to save Mrs. Cut-Cut, if it was His will.

"Fay, Jerry," Mother called from the side porch. "It is time to hunt for the eggs."

"All right," they answered.

Hunting for the eggs was Fay and Jerry's job in the middle of the morning.

Mother always said, "When hens stop cackling loudly and begin to cluck quietly, then it is time to hunt the eggs."

Most of the hens laid their eggs in the nests in the henhouse. But others liked to lay outside. The children had found many of these outside nests by watching from the Lookout.

They did not pay any **attention** to a hen if she were just scratching around looking for bugs and worms.

But when they heard one cackling loudly,

they looked to see where she had come from. Then down they would run to where the hen had been.

Sometimes they had to hunt around a while before they found the nest. But most of the time they found a warm, new egg.

Fay and Jerry knew all the places where hens laid their eggs outside. It did not take long to get the eggs and carry them into the house.

"May we go back to the Lookout?" Fay asked Mother.

"Yes, I don't have anything for you to do right now," said Mother, "but I will need you a little later. I will need you to pick the feathers off that old white hen as soon as Daddy has time to cut off her head."

Fay and Jerry said nothing. They went out and ran up to the Lookout.

"Oh, Jerry, what shall we do?" cried Fay.

"I guess we had better pray again," said Jerry.

So again they prayed. They asked God to save Mrs. Cut-Cut from being made into chicken potpie.

Then they just sat there, sadly looking out over the world.

Suddenly Jerry said, "Fay, I saw something move down there at the hay bales. Something white."

"Where?" asked Fay. "The bales are white. I can't see anything."

Jerry jumped up. "Come," he cried. "I think it might be Mrs. Cut-Cut. Maybe she has a nest down there."

Down out of the barn they flew. In no time they were over the fence at the row of hay bales.

There came Mrs. Cut-Cut walking toward them, picking bugs off the weeds as she came.

"Cut-cut-cut-ca-dah-ca," she cackled, as if to say, "What are you two doing down here?"

For once, Fay and Jerry did not talk to the white hen. They did not pay any attention to their pet now. They were sure. Oh, yes, they were sure that God had answered their prayers.

They began looking on the ground between the bales.

"I saw her here, I think," said Jerry, in great excitement. "No. It must have been here, between these two."

"We'll have to look between all of the bales," Fay said. "Maybe we should start at the end of the row."

But just then Jerry cried, "Here it is! Oh, Fay, come look at all the eggs!"

There between two of the big white bales was a nest full of white eggs laid by a fat white hen.

"There must be a dozen there," cried Fay. "They won't all be good to eat, but let's go tell Mother."

The children began to run toward the house. On the way they met a fat white hen scratching in the grass.

"You are saved, Mrs. Cut-Cut," cried Fay. "God saved you just in time. What a close call!"

"Daddy thought you were a good layer," said Jerry. "And he was right."

"Cut-cut-cut-ca-dah-ca," cackled Mrs. Cut-Cut, as if to say, "Of course, I'm a good layer. I always have been."

Then she went on scratching.

– Leah Kauffman Lind

You will enjoy these two poems. One is about a rooster. The other tells the very best way to get help when you don't know what to do.

Chanticleer

High and proud on the barnyard fence
Walks rooster in the morning.
He shakes his comb, he shakes his tail,
And gives his daily warning.

"Get up, you lazy boys
    and girls,
It's time you should
    be dressing!"
I wonder if he
    keeps a clock,
Or if he's only
    guessing.

– *John Farrar*

A Good Plan

When you don't know what to do,
Can't tell which way's right for you,
    Pray to God a prayer.
He will have an answer true,
God will tell you what to do;
    God is everywhere.

He will help you choose the way,
In your work and in your play;
    God is everywhere.
So if you are in doubt some day
And need help to choose the way,
    Pray to God a prayer.

–Author Unknown

"Blessed are the peacemakers."
—Matthew 5:9

Enemy or Peacemaker?

*Why was Josie willing to be
friends again so soon?*

Molly went into the house. She sat down in the kitchen. She looked cross and ready to cry.

Mother was looking in the freezer. She was looking to see if the **homemade** ice cream was frozen yet.

"It is almost hard enough to eat. It will be

just right by lunchtime," she said.

She put down the lid of the freezer and turned around. "Why, Molly. Where is Jolly Josie?" Jolly **Josie** was the name Molly had given her best friend.

"She went home," said Molly.

"So soon? She wasn't here very long."

"I know. She got mad at me, so she went home."

"What did you do?" asked Mother.

"I didn't do anything. But she said I did."

"Tell me what happened."

"We were playing tag. We were running in and out of the gate.

"Josie had a dime in her dress pocket. She lost it. It hopped out of her pocket somewhere. We looked and looked for it, but didn't find it.

"Then she blamed me. She said it was my

fault because I was chasing her."

"What did you say?" asked Mother.

"Well, she made me cross. I said, 'That's silly. It **probably** hopped out when you were chasing *me*.' That's when she got mad and went home.

"She was crying too, because the dime was for an ice cream cone. Her mother was taking her to the store after lunch.

"Her mother had said it would be best to leave the dime at home. But Josie wanted to show it to me, so she brought it.

"She knew her mother would be cross at her, so she blamed me. She said I made her lose it. And she said she wasn't ever going to play with me again.

"But it wasn't my fault, was it, Mother?"

"No, Molly. It wasn't your fault. But do you want Josie to be your **enemy**? Wouldn't you like to be friends with her again?"

"I guess so," said Molly slowly. "She is the only girl my age around here. We always have the best times. There wouldn't be anyone to play with if I didn't have Jolly Josie." Molly was almost crying.

"Jesus said, 'Blessed are the **peacemakers**,' so you would be happy if you made peace with Josie," said Mother.

"He also said that if your enemy is hungry, you should feed him. Since Josie can't buy any ice cream, maybe you want to feed her with some of the ice cream I am making. Homemade ice cream is better than what you buy at the store. It will be ready soon after lunch. Do you want to try to get Josie feeling jolly again?"

"I guess I could try," said Molly slowly. "But she should be the peacemaker. She started the fuss. What would I say?"

Mother smiled. "You might say, 'Here comes the peacemaker, coming to feed her enemy.'"

Molly laughed. "Oh, Mother, I'd better not say that. Josie might get mad all over again."

"Well, Jesus will give you the right words when you get there," said Mother. "After lunch we will fix up two dishes of ice cream. You can carry them over. Josie will get some ice cream even if she did lose her dime.

"You may not need to say much. The ice cream will tell Josie what you mean."

"Maybe it will," agreed Molly. "I'll try it."

After lunch, Mother and Molly got two pretty blue dishes. They put a heap of the pink homemade ice cream in each. They put a red cherry on the top.

"Aren't they pretty?" said Molly. "If this doesn't make Josie feel jolly, I'll bring them back. You and I can eat them.

"You know, Mother," she went on, "I'm feeling happy already. I think planning to be a peacemaker is fun."

Molly had a little smile on her face as she

started for Josie's house. When she got to the gate she pushed it open. And there, close to the gate post, she saw the lost dime.

She set one dish in the grass and put the dime into her dress pocket. When she picked up the dish from the grass her smile was bigger than ever.

Molly went around Josie's house to the side porch. There sat her friend on the swing. She did not look a bit jolly.

Molly didn't even think about what to say. She went up the steps and held out a dish of ice cream.

"Here, Josie," she said, just as if nothing had happened. "You don't need to go buy ice cream. Mother just made some. I like this kind. She puts **strawberry** jelly in it."

Josie took the dish. She slid over to make room for Molly.

"Thank you," she said quietly. "The cherry

looks pretty on the pink ice cream. Strawberry is the kind I like best."

Then Molly started to laugh. "Oh, Josie, I forgot spoons. Shall we just lick it like ice cream cones?"

A little smile came on Josie's face. "No, I'll get spoons." She got off the swing and went into the house. When she came out with spoons she looked a lot more like Jolly Josie.

The girls began to eat.

"M-m-m-m-m-m-m, this is good," said Josie, licking at her first spoonful. "But what I want to know is why you brought it over. After what I said to you, I was afraid you wouldn't want to talk to me for weeks. I'm sorry I blamed you, Molly. The whole thing was my fault."

"Well, I sure wasn't happy when you got mad at me," Molly said. "But I didn't want to be your enemy. And Mother said I would be happy if I tried to be a peacemaker. So I tried it and it worked."

Josie smiled. And now she looked even more like Jolly Josie. "Wasn't it silly of me to get mad over a little thing like a dime?"

"Oh, I forgot," cried Molly. "Look what I found coming over here!" She pulled out the dime.

Josie's mouth fell open. "You mean you found it without even looking! After the way we hunted for it!"

"Yes, it was lying there in the grass by the post."

"You know what I think?" said Josie. "I think Jesus showed you where it was because you were coming over to be a peacemaker."

"Probably He did," said the little peacemaker. "Probably He did."

– Grace Cash

> *"Thou shalt not bow down thyself to them,*
> *nor serve them."* —Exodus 20:5

Letter From an Indian Missionary

How did this story make you feel?

Dear Boys and Girls,

In this letter I want to tell you a little about the country of India.

India is far across the sea. India is the country that **Columbus** thought he had reached when his ships came to our country.

That is why he called the people Indians. But at that time Columbus did not know that India was really halfway around the world from where he was.

The true Indians are the people who live in India. That country is thousands of miles from our country.

Millions and millions of people live in India. Most of them are very poor. Most of them do not know about Jesus.

I went to India in 1900. That was long before you or your daddy and mother were born. It was before your grandpa and grandma were born.

When I was in India, the people did not live as we do today. They dressed in different clothes. They lived in different kinds of houses. They ate different kinds of food. They even ate their food in a different way than we do. They did not use spoons and forks. They ate neatly with the tips of their fingers.

One time at a train **station,** I saw a little family—a father, mother, and three children. They were waiting for a train.

It was dinnertime. They had their dinner with them. Their dinner was a pot of rice with another dish of meat gravy.

The little family sat on the ground around their pot of rice close to the train station.

Wide green leaves were the plates. The mother put a little pile of rice on each leaf.

Then with the tips of their thumbs and fingers they rolled bits of rice into balls. They dipped the balls in the gravy and popped them into their mouths. You and I could never have done it so neatly.

All around them hundreds of people were coming and going. But the little family sat and ate their dinner as happily as if they were at home.

I also saw things in India that made me very sad. Most of the people do not know and love Jesus. They worship animals. The cow is one of the animals they think is **holy.** They will starve to death before they will kill a cow for food.

One time I saw a dirty old cow coming down the middle of the street. The street was not very wide. Everyone got out of the cow's way because they thought it was holy.

Then an old man ran in front of the cow as she **plodded** along. I saw him kneel down and fold his hands in prayer to the cow. He bent his head to the ground two or three times in front of the old cow.

The cow did not even look at the man as she plodded on. The man got up from his knees to let her pass. But she did not pay any attention to him.

It made me want to cry to see him praying to a dirty old cow that did not even look at him. I wanted to tell him about our wonderful,

loving God. I wanted to tell him about our God who listens when we pray to Him, and who answers our prayers.

I wanted to tell him about our loving God who sent His Son to die for him and take away his sins.

Boys and girls, will you pray for the millions in India who do not know Jesus? Will you pray that they might hear the Good News about the One who came to save them from their sins?

With love, your missionary friend from India.

Uncle Jake

The old man in the story bowed down to a cow because he did not know about the heavenly Father.

The poem tells two things a robin saw people doing. He asked the sparrow why they did them. The sparrow told the robin what he thought. Do you think the sparrow was right?

Overheard in an Orchard

Said the Robin to the Sparrow:
   "I should really like to know
Why these anxious human beings
   Rush about and worry so."

Said the Sparrow to the Robin:
   "Friend, I think that it must be
That they have no heavenly Father
   Such as cares for you and me."

–Elizabeth Cheney

"I have chosen the way of truth."

−Psalm 119:30

A Chance for This and a Chance for That

Eric was sure he knew what Nathan had done and why he had done it. Was he right?

Bang! Eric slammed the door behind him.

Bang! He dropped his lunch box on the **counter**.

Bang! He slapped his books on the table.

"Eric Carter," said his mother. "That is enough of that. What has upset you?"

"That new boy! That old Nathan Ball!"

"Nathan? Yesterday you said he was going to be your best friend."

"That was yesterday. But not today!"

"What did you do?"

"I didn't do anything. It's what he did. His father has a big boat. And all the boys in our grade got an **invitation** from Nathan to go on a boat ride. They are going up the river for a picnic tomorrow. All but me!"

"Did you hear him invite all the others?"

"No. He sent them notes in the mail. Everyone was talking about it in school today."

"There must be some **mistake**," said Mother. "He would not have left you out. Maybe there isn't room on the boat for all of you boys."

"Yes, there is. Nathan told me it holds ten. There are only six of us boys."

"I still think there is some mistake," said

Mother. "Did you say anything to him about it?"

"Well, I guess not!" said Eric. "He left me out just to be mean. He watched me all day, to see how I was taking it.

"I'm going to look for a chance to get even with him. Then I'll watch *him* to see how *he* is taking it. Just you wait! I'll think of something!" Eric's face was red. He talked loudly.

"Eric," said Mother quietly. "Do you know why you are talking like this?"

"I sure do! It is because Nathan is so mean!"

"No, Eric. You are talking like this because you were not invited to the picnic.

I don't blame you for feeling hurt. But if Nathan did this because he was feeling mean, you will have to do something just as mean to get even with him, won't you?"

Eric said nothing. Mother was right. He was deeply hurt over what Nathan had done. The new boy had seemed so nice. Eric knew he was acting angry to keep from crying.

"Being angry is wrong. Trying to get even is wrong," said Mother. "You know what the Bible says about that."

"But I don't feel like being nice to him. I wish I could plan a picnic. I'd leave him out so he'd know how it feels!"

"That would not make you happy," said Mother. "Sit down here and eat that last piece of lemon pie on the counter. Try to think of something nice to do for Nathan. If you keep your eyes open, you will get an **opportunity** to do him a good turn."

Eric got the lemon pie from the counter. As he pulled out a chair, Mother said, "You know Jesus really does mean for us to return good for evil. So you will have to keep that in mind. Be on the lookout for a chance to do Nathan a good turn.

"That is the only way to help you feel right toward him. The sooner you do it the better."

"But I won't have a chance to do anything until Monday. And that will be too late, because the picnic is tomorrow."

"Do you think the Bible tells us to return good for evil so things turn out nice for us?"

Eric didn't say anything. He knew the answer to that.

"I'll try to think of something too," said Mother.

Yes, Eric knew his mother would try to think of something. She would keep after him until he felt right toward Nathan. She would keep after him until he had done Nathan a good turn of some kind. That's the way his mother was.

He ate the lemon pie. It helped. But in his heart he hoped the opportunity to do Nathan a good turn would not come for a long time. Years maybe. What he wanted right now was a chance to get even.

After supper, Eric went out to feed his dog and tie him up for the night. There, playing with Jock, was Nathan's new little puppy. It must have tagged along with Jock when he made his evening run around town.

Here was his chance to get even! A new puppy in a new town! It would never find its way home by itself. It might even get run over! Puppies didn't have enough sense to stay off the street. It would serve Nathan right if he never saw his dog again!

I wouldn't have to do anything! I could just tie Jock and let the puppy go where it pleased, he thought.

But then Eric had another thought.

Here, also, was his chance to do Nathan a good turn. He didn't need his mother to tell him that!

Two chances! A chance to get even.

A chance to do Nathan a good turn. Which one should he take?

It took Eric a long time to tie up Jock. He was thinking hard.

At last he picked up the puppy. "Might as well get it over with," he said to himself. "But it won't make me feel any better toward him even if it is a good turn. At least it will show Mother I did what she said."

As Eric turned the corner into Nathan's street he heard someone calling, "Here, Pudgie! Here, Pudgie!" Then three sharp whistles. Nathan was coming toward him looking for his puppy.

Eric stopped and waited until Nathan came up. "Is this what you are looking for?"

he asked, holding out the puppy.

"Oh, Eric! Am I ever glad you found him!" cried Nathan. "I was afraid he was lost for good! He's not used to our new place yet. He might have gotten run over. Puppies don't have sense enough to stay off the street."

"I know," said Eric. He couldn't think of anything else to say. He turned to go.

"Well—" said Nathan. "Well, I'll see you tomorrow."

Eric's mouth dropped open. "Tomorrow? Where?"

"On the boat, of course. Aren't you coming?"

"The boat? I don't go where I'm not invited," said Eric stiffly. Why was Nathan acting like he had invited him?

"What do you mean, 'not invited'?" cried

Nathan. "Your invitation was the first one I wrote. After all, you are my best friend!"

"You didn't send me any invitation."

"I did so! I remember writing, 'Eric Carter, 59 River Street.'"

"River Street! We don't live on River Street! We live on Water Street! That's a long way from River Street!"

"You mean you didn't get my note? I thought you didn't want to come with me. I kept watching you today, hoping you'd say something. But you never did. You'll come, won't you?"

Eric laughed a joyous laugh. "Of course I'll come if you want me.

"Now I have to run. My mother doesn't know I came over here. She'll be glad when I tell her. That's one thing I know!"

–Marion Ullmark

Which Loved Her Best?

"I love you, Mother," said little John,
Then forgetting his work, his cap went on,
And he was off to the garden swing,
Leaving his mother the wood to bring.

"I love you, Mother," said little Nell,
"I love you better than tongue can tell."
Then she teased and pouted full half the day,
Till Mother rejoiced when she went to play.

"I love you, Mother," said little Fan,
"Today I'll help you all I can.
"How glad I am that school doesn't keep."
So she rocked the babe till it fell asleep.

Then stepping softly, she took the broom,
And swept the floor, and dusted the room;
Busy and happy all day was she,
Helpful and cheerful as child could be.

"I love you, Mother," again they said—
Three little children going to bed.
How do you think that Mother guessed
Which of them really loved her best?

— Joy Allison

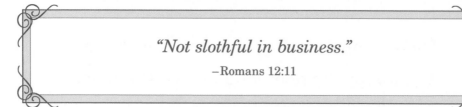

"Not slothful in business."

–Romans 12:11

The Mystery Stone

Was everyone in the story slothful?

Long, long ago there was a king who loved his people. He tried to help them love each other and have good habits. "Bad things in life come to the lazy and careless and selfish," he told them. "Good things come to the busy workers who are helpful to others."

One night he put a large stone in the middle of the road near his **palace**. He wanted to see what his people would do with it. Would they be too lazy to move it?

Or would they move it so the road would be clear for everyone? Then he went back to his palace to watch what would happen.

Early the next morning a farmer named Peter came along. He was driving a heavy **oxcart**. He had to stop when he came to the stone. He got down and looked at it. "Now this is a **mystery**," he said.

"Where did this big stone come from? Why haven't the lazy people of this town taken it out of the road? I'd be **ashamed** to be so lazy. Now I must drive my oxcart out on the grass to get around it."

And that is what he did. Then he went on his way, **scolding** about the lazy people in the town.

Next came a young man singing a merry song. He was on his way to work. He was looking at the sky and the birds.

He held his head so high that he did not

see the stone. He fell over it. Down into the dust he went. That put an end to his merry song. He got up. He brushed off the dust and began to scold.

"Where did this big stone come from? What lazy people there are around here! They have no more sense than to leave a big stone in the middle of the road. They should be ashamed of themselves."

He went on his way, but he did not sing again.

Along came six **merchants**. They had large wagons full of goods to sell in the town. When they came to the stone, they drove out on the grass and went around it. The mystery stone made them angry too. They, too, began scolding.

"Did you ever see the like?" they cried. "A big stone in the middle of the road, and everyone is too lazy to move it! Who put it here? Whoever it was should take it off the road."

It was market day. More than fifty people went by the stone on their way to market that day. But no one stopped to move it out of the road. Everyone was carrying something or was too busy or too lazy to stop. And the king watched from his palace.

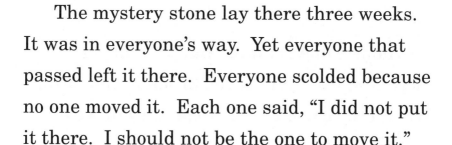

The mystery stone lay there three weeks. It was in everyone's way. Yet everyone that passed left it there. Everyone scolded because no one moved it. Each one said, "I did not put it there. I should not be the one to move it."

One day the king sent word to all the people. Everyone should go to the place where the stone lay in the middle of the road.

Farmer Peter came. The young working man came. The six merchants came. And all the other people who had been walking around the stone came too.

"I hope the king will find out what a lazy set of people he has in this town," said Peter. "I hope he finds out who put that stone in the middle of the road."

"So do I," said the young man.

"So do I," cried each of the six merchants.

"Yes, yes," cried all the other people.

Just then they heard the sound of a horn. The king was coming from his palace!

He rode up to the mystery stone and got down from his horse. All the people became very quiet.

"My good people," he said. "For three weeks I have watched you passing along this road. I have seen you going out on the grass to get around this stone. I have heard you scolding about the lazy people who have not

moved the stone. Every one of you has seen
it, but every one of you has left it where it is.
Every one of you has scolded everyone else for
not moving it."

Then the king stooped down and rolled the
stone over. Under it, in a hole, lay a box.

The king picked up the box. A paper was tied
to it. The king read what was on the paper.

FOR HIM WHO MOVES THE STONE.

He opened the box and turned it upside
down. Out fell fifty bright gold coins.

"Now you see what any one of you could
have had if you had not been so lazy and selfish.
You would have had this money. You would
have helped all the people who passed this way.

"None of you wanted to move the stone
because you had not put it there. Each of you
scolded because others were too lazy to move it.
But every one of you was lazy.

"I, your king, put the stone here. I wanted to show you that good things come to people who are not lazy. Good things come to those who try to be helpful to others. Now you may go."

Farmer Peter, the young workman, the six merchants, and all the people went away with their heads bowed. How ashamed they all were. They had learned a lesson they would not soon forget.

– An old tale

The way of traveling in this poem is far different from the ways of travel in the story you just read.

Taking Off

The airplane taxis down the field
And heads into the breeze,
It lifts its wheels above the ground,
It skims above the trees,
It rises high and higher
Away up toward the sun,
It's just a speck against the sky—
  And now it's gone!

—*Mary Green*

The Fall of Jericho

1. Now **Jericho** was straitly shut up because of the children of **Israel**: none went out, and none came in.

2. And the LORD said unto **Joshua**, See, I have given into thine hand Jericho, and the king thereof, and the mighty men of **valour**.

3. And ye shall **compass** the city, all ye men of war, and go round about the city once. Thus shalt thou do six days.

4. And seven priests shall bear before the **ark** seven **trumpets** of rams' horns: and the seventh day ye shall compass the city seven times, and the priests shall blow with the trumpets.

5. And it shall come to pass, that when they make a long blast with the ram's horn, and when ye hear the sound of the trumpet, all the people shall shout with a great

shout; and the wall of the city shall fall down flat, and the people shall **ascend** up every man straight before him.

6. And Joshua the son of Nun called the priests, and said unto them, Take up the ark of the **covenant**, and let seven priests bear seven trumpets of rams' horns before the ark of the Lord.

7. And he said unto the people, Pass on, and compass the city, and let him that is armed pass on before the ark of the Lord.

8. And it came to pass, when Joshua had spoken unto the people, that the seven priests bearing the seven trumpets of rams' horns passed on before the Lord, and blew with the trumpets: and the ark of the covenant of the Lord followed them.

9. And the armed men went before the priests that blew with the trumpets, and the **rereward** came after the ark,

the priests going on, and blowing with the trumpets.

10. And Joshua had commanded the people, saying, Ye shall not shout, nor make any noise with your voice, neither shall any word proceed out of your mouth, until the day I bid you shout; then shall ye shout.

11. So the ark of the LORD compassed the city, going about it once: and they came into the camp, and lodged in the camp.

12. And Joshua rose early in the morning, and the priests took up the ark of the LORD.

13. And seven priests bearing seven trumpets of rams' horns before the ark of the LORD went on continually, and blew with the trumpets: and the armed men went before them; but the rereward came after the ark of the LORD, the priests going on, and blowing with the trumpets.

14. And the second day they compassed the

city once, and returned into the camp: so they did six days.

15. And it came to pass on the seventh day, that they rose early about the dawning of the day, and compassed the city after the same manner seven times: only on that day they compassed the city seven times.

16. And it came to pass at the seventh time, when the priests blew with the trumpets, Joshua said unto the people, Shout; for the Lord hath given you the city.

20. So the people shouted when the priests blew with the trumpets: and it came to pass, when the people heard the sound of the trumpet, and the people shouted with a great shout, that the wall fell down flat, so that the people went up into the city, every man straight before him, and they took the city.

– Joshua 6:1-16, 20

"And as ye would that men should do to you, do ye also to them likewise." –Luke 6:31

Golden Rule Corn

What is your answer to the question on page 242?

When the sweet corn was ripe, Father made a big sign. Mother painted the words on it. Father **posted** the sign by the road at the end of the lane.

The sign said, **SWEET CORN FOR SALE.**

Father set many baskets of corn **beneath** the big tree in the front yard.

Benny sat on the swing. He hoped people would see the sign and come in to buy corn.

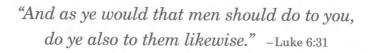

Soon a blue car slowed down. The man was looking at the sign. Then he turned in the lane.

Benny ran to the house. "Mother, a man is coming for corn," he cried.

Mother wiped her hands on her **apron**. She came out on the porch as the man came up.

"You have sweet corn for sale, Ma'am?"

"Yes, we do," answered Mother.

The man went over to the baskets under the tree. He looked at the ears of corn. "I'll take a **dozen** ears, please."

Benny watched Mother take a paper bag. She began to put ears of corn into it. He counted as she put them in. One, two, three, four, five, six, seven, eight, nine, ten, eleven, twelve, thirteen.

Thirteen! Benny looked at Mother. She

had made a mistake. She had put in thirteen ears instead of twelve.

The man paid Mother. He took the bag of corn and drove out the lane.

"Mother, you didn't count right," said Benny. "You gave the man thirteen ears of corn instead of twelve. I counted as you put them in."

"So you counted, did you?" said Mother with a smile. "Well, I wanted to give him thirteen. I meant to give him an **extra** one."

"Why, Mother? He paid for only a dozen."

"I know, but Father and I want everyone to be happy with the corn they buy from us. Sometimes there might be a bad ear or one that is smaller. An extra one will make up for any that might not be good."

"But we won't get as much money that way," said Benny. "If we give thirteen ears instead of twelve, then—then . . ." Benny was thinking hard. "Then after twelve people buy a dozen ears, that would be the same as giving away a whole dozen without getting paid for it."

"That's right, Benny."

"But if we sell all these baskets of corn, look how much money we will lose."

"I know we won't get quite as much money," said Mother. "But money is not the first thing we should think about.

"God wants His children to be unselfish and kind even when they don't make quite as much money as they could. Jesus said we should do to others as we would want others to do to us."

"That's the Golden Rule, isn't it?" said Benny.

"Yes," said Mother. "If we were buying corn we would be happy for an extra ear. So we give an extra ear."

"I see," said Benny. But he wasn't sure about it. It seemed to him that the only ones who could be happy with the Golden Rule would be the ones who got the extra corn. How can you be happy giving corn away without getting any money for it?

Then he looked out the lane. "Here come two more cars," he cried.

The two cars drove up. A lady got out of each one. They came over to the tree.

One lady said, "I saw your sign. I will take three dozen ears, please."

Mother looked at the other lady.

"I'll take one dozen," she said.

That is four free ears that we won't get paid for, thought Benny.

Mother picked up two bags. She gave one to Benny. "Will you please count out a dozen for this lady, Benny?"

"Oh, yes," said Benny. He took the bag and

began to put in ears of corn. One, two, three . . . on up to thirteen, just as Mother wanted him to do. But he didn't feel too good about it.

The lady was watching him. She said, "I think you put in one ear too many. You gave me thirteen."

"I meant to do that," said Benny. "We give everyone thirteen ears instead of twelve. That's in case one ear is bad or is smaller."

The lady smiled a big smile. "How nice of you. Not many people would do that."

Now Benny smiled too. He began to feel better.

"Mother said we want to follow the Golden Rule the way Jesus told us to."

"That is wonderful! You people must be Christians."

"Yes, we are," said Mother.

"This is the nicest thing that has happened to me for a long time. People like you make the world a happier place. Thank you so much. And you too, Benny."

The other lady said, "Yes, thank you for the extra ears. I will tell my friends that this is the place to come for corn. I am glad to have met you. Thanks again."

Benny watched the two cars drive out the lane.

"They were nice, weren't they?" he said.

"Do you know why?" asked Mother.

"I guess it was because they got extra ears of corn."

"I don't think so," said Mother. "They didn't get all that much extra corn. The extra ears just showed we were thinking of them before ourselves. Being kind and unselfish always makes others happy."

"Jesus must have known that when He gave us the Golden Rule," said Benny.

"I am sure He did."

"And you know, Mother, when they talked so nice and acted so happy, that made me feel happy too. That's funny. I thought only the people who got the extra corn would be happy when we followed the Golden Rule.

"Do you think Jesus knew the Golden Rule would work that way too?"

"I am sure He did. But you had to give the extra ear of corn before you found that out," said Mother.

"I know. And it's fun," said Benny. "And here comes another car."

–Mary Hursh

Andy's Real Question

What was Andy's real question?

Andy was not very big, but he had a big question. His mother would know the answer. He went down the **basement** steps. She was washing the clothes.

"Mother, where is God?" Andy watched Mother out of the corner of his eye. He hoped she wouldn't laugh at his question.

Mother did not laugh, not the least little bit.

"God is in Heaven," she said.

"Oh," said Andy. That's all he said out loud. But he was thinking about what he really wanted to know. *If God is in Heaven, how can He hear when I pray?*

Mother had not answered his real question.

Andy ran up the basement steps. Grandmother was in the kitchen washing dishes.

"Grandmother, where is God?"

"Well, Andy, you know why we go to church. The church is God's house. He is there whenever we go to church."

"Oh," said Andy. Now he was **confused** for sure! If God were in Heaven, how could He be in church too? The church was far away from their house. How could God hear him when he prayed, if He were way over at the church?

Grandmother had not answered his real

question either.

Andy went into the living room. Daddy was at his desk in the corner reading his Bible.

"Daddy, where is God?"

Daddy didn't laugh, not a single little bit.

"God is right here in this room," he said softly.

"Oh," said Andy. "Then why did Mother say He is up in Heaven? And why did Grandmother say He is in church?"

"Because He is. God is in Heaven and in church and right in this room with us too."

"All those places? All at the same time?" asked Andy.

"Yes," said Daddy.

"How can He be?"

"Well, Andy, God is different from you and me. We can be at only one place at one time.

But God is everywhere all the time.

"He takes care of His people on this side of the world. He takes care of His people on the other side of the world. Day and night He sees us and takes care of us all."

"How can He?" asked Andy.

Daddy shook his head. "I do not know. No one knows. No one can **explain** it."

"Then how do we know He can be in all those places at the same time?" asked Andy. He felt very sad. No one could answer his real question.

But Daddy said, "That's easy. The Bible tells us. That's how we know."

Daddy began to turn the pages of his Bible.

"Listen to this verse, Andy. I'm not going to read the whole verse. Just parts of it, to show that God is in Heaven."

Then Daddy read, " 'If my people ... shall **humble** themselves, and pray ... then will I hear from heaven.'

"That's why Mother said God is in Heaven."

Daddy turned more pages. "Listen to this, 'For where two or three are **gathered** together in my name, there am I in the **midst** of them.'

"That's how Grandmother knows God is in church when we go there to worship."

Daddy kept turning pages. Then he stopped and said, "This next verse will be a little hard for you to understand. But listen to what Jesus told His **disciples**, 'If a man love me, he will keep my words; and my Father will love him, and we will come unto him, and make our **abode** with him.' "

Daddy swung around from the desk and faced Andy. "That means if we do what Jesus tells us, He and His Father, God, will come and live in our hearts. And that's how I know God is right here with us now."

"Oh," said Andy. He smiled a big smile. "Thank you, Daddy. Now I see how God can be at all those places at the same time. Well, I don't really see how He can, but since the Bible says so, that's the way it is."

Then Andy ran away to his room where he could think things over by himself.

At last his real question was answered. The very first verse Daddy had read had told him what he really wanted to know.

Now he knew that when he prayed, God heard him way, way, way up there in heaven.

And Andy was glad.

– Edna Beiler

> *"My son, hear the instruction of thy father, and forsake not the law of thy mother."* –Proverbs 1:8

Mario and the Monkeys

A Story from South America

Could this story have happened where you live?

Mario and his parents lived in a little **cottage**. It was far away, in a great forest in South America. They were very poor. His father worked hard on their little farm.

Mother made doll clothes to sell. Mario would take them to the **marketplace** in town. He had to walk along a hot, dusty road to get to town.

Sometimes he would go through the forest. It was longer that way, but he liked it better. The trees were filled with **huge** butterflies and singing birds. **Chattering** monkeys made Mario laugh as he watched them swinging from branch to branch above his head.

One morning, Mario's mother came from the cottage to where he was sitting in the shade. She said it was time to sell the doll hats she had made. She packed a lunch for Mario. She put the lunch in the bottom of a big basket. On top of the lunch she put the doll hats.

"Now be very careful," she said. "Keep your eye on the hats. Do not let anything happen to them."

"I will be very careful. I will get them to the market in fine shape," Mario said. "Good-bye, Mother."

He took the big basket of doll hats and started for the market in town.

The day was very hot, so he took the **trail** through the forest. It was cool under the shady trees.

As he walked along, Mario laughed at the chattering monkeys. He watched them swing along in the trees above his head.

After a while it was time to eat his lunch. Mario sat down in the cool shade under a big tree. He took out the doll hats and carefully laid them on the grass. Mother had packed a big lunch. How good it tasted. Mario ate every bit of it.

He brushed the crumbs from his clothes. Then he sat and watched the monkeys.

And they watched him. But Mario did not keep his eye on the doll hats. He forgot all about them. It was so warm. Mario was tired. Soon he nodded. He put his head against the huge tree trunk and fell asleep with his hat over his eyes.

The monkeys in the treetops sat still. They watched for a long time. When the boy did not move, they slowly began to come down from the trees.

Slowly they came close to Mario. Still he did not move. The monkeys picked up the crumbs from Mario's lunch. They sniffed at the doll hats.

They looked from the doll hats to Mario with his hat on his head. One monkey picked up a doll hat and put it on his head. The next moment all the monkeys wore hats.

Up the tree they ran. They began to play. Through the branches they chased each other.

They chattered until they woke Mario.

The boy opened his eyes and pushed back

his hat. Then he saw
the monkeys.

"The doll hats! My
mother's doll hats,"
he cried, jumping up.
"Give them back!"

But the monkeys
only chattered down at
him as if to say, "Come
and get them if you can."

"What can I do?"
Mario asked himself.
"Mother told me to keep
my eye on the doll hats,
but I went to sleep.
Now how can I get
them away from those
monkeys?"

Suddenly, Mario thought
of something his father had told him. Monkeys
are copycats. They copy what people do."

"If monkeys are copycats," Mario said to
himself. "I'll see if they copy me."

Taking off his hat, Mario threw it on the
grass. Nothing happened. He picked up his
hat and threw it down again.

Then a doll hat fell through the leaves of the tree. Down came another and another until all the hats lay on the grass at Mario's feet.

The boy picked them up one by one. He looked at each one carefully as he put it into the basket. They were not hurt at all. Laughing happily, Mario waved good-bye to the chattering monkeys. Then he started down the trail toward the town.

As he sold the hats in the marketplace, he thought, *The dolls will never know that monkeys wore these hats before they did.*

–A South American Folk Tale

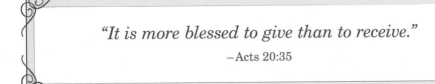

"It is more blessed to give than to receive."

—Acts 20:35

The Stolen Popsicle

Part 1

*Why didn't Toby like to put money in
the basket at Sunday school?*

On the way home from school on Monday, Toby stopped at the ice cream store.

He laid the quarter on the counter. "What kind of **popsicles** do you have?" he asked the little man.

"Cherry, orange, strawberry, grape, and lemon."

Toby thought a little. "Make it orange, please," he said. He pushed the quarter across the counter. He didn't really care which flavor he got. He liked them all. And the **wrappers** were all worth just as much.

He always bought a popsicle when he had money. You could get prizes if you saved the wrappers and sent them in.

Of course, he liked popsicles. Any flavor. Winter or summer, spring or fall, Toby would buy a popsicle if he had a quarter and Mother let him spend it.

This time he had not asked her about spending it. She did not know he had a quarter.

Outside the store, Toby broke the popsicle in half. He left one half in the wrapper and put it into his pocket. The other half he put to his lips and **sucked.** M-m-m-m-m-m-m-m. How sweet and cold and good it was!

This was better than putting the quarter in the basket at Sunday school. He was glad he had not done that.

Toby started on toward home, sucking on the popsicle. After a while he began to step on the cracks in the sidewalk. It was a game he played with himself. He tried to step on every crack. He counted them as he went. He hoped to get to a hundred sometime. But he never had yet. The rule was if you missed one, you had to start over. And if you forgot what number you were on, you had to start over.

Of course, it didn't matter if he did miss or forget where he was. It was just a game.

But Mother had said she would give him a quarter for a popsicle if he ever got to a hundred. So whenever he was walking by himself, he always made an **attempt** to reach a hundred.

Right now, he was up to forty-seven, and the first half of his popsicle was gone.

Toby stopped. He threw the stick away and pulled out the other half. It was getting a little **slushy**.

He smoothed the wrapper. Then he folded it and put it into his pocket. That was one more for his **collection**.

The popsicle began to drip, so he had to eat it fast. As he sucked on the sweet, slushy popsicle, he thought about the quarter he had just spent.

Daddy had given it to him to put in the basket at Sunday school. But he had kept it instead. When the basket came around the class, he just passed it on.

Toby had felt kind of funny passing on the basket like that. But the minute he thought of popsicles, he stopped feeling funny. Instead, he started feeling excited and happy.

He could get a popsicle on the way home from school tomorrow. Daddy had given him the quarter, so it was his money, wasn't it? It wasn't as if he had stolen it.

Somehow Toby had never liked to put money into that basket at Sunday school. The teacher called it their class collection money. But he never knew what it went for. When he gave money, he liked to see what he was getting.

Like today. When he put down his quarter in the ice cream store, he got a popsicle right then. That's the way Toby liked to spend his money.

"Let's see," he said to himself. "If Daddy gives me a quarter every Sunday, and I keep it, I can get a popsicle every week. By Christmas I'll have a pile of wrappers."

Toby didn't know how many wrappers he would have by that time. But he was sure he would have enough to send off for one of the prizes.

Toby ate the rest of the slushy popsicle; then went on stepping on the cracks and counting. Soon he forgot about popsicles and wrappers. He forgot about the quarter he had not put into the Sunday school basket. He was getting close home and had not missed one crack. He was in the eighties! Never before had he gotten so close to a hundred. Maybe this time he would make it! Wouldn't that be something to tell Mother when he got home! And she would give him a quarter for another popsicle!

Toby turned into his own yard. He was at ninety-four. He stopped and looked up the front walk. He counted the cracks. There were five. That would put him only to ninety-nine!

Toby could hardly believe he had gotten so close to a hundred. But he wouldn't be able to make it.

"Why didn't I start counting sooner—way back there as soon as I came out of the store? Here I am, almost to a hundred for the first time in my life. Now I've run out of cracks!"

"I know what I'll do," he said at last. "When I am on the last crack at the bottom of the steps, I'll make one jump up onto the porch. If I land on the mat, I'll count that for a hundred. That will be fair, because jumping up three steps onto the mat is harder than stepping on a crack. I'll ask Mother if that would count for a crack."

Toby stood at the bottom of the steps. He took a good look at how far it was from there to the mat on the porch.

"I can do it," he said.

Toby stepped back a little way. Then he took a running start and jumped.

—*Milo Kauffman*

> *"Let him that stole steal no more ... that he may have to give to him that needeth."* –Ephesians 4:28

The Stolen Popsicle

Part 2

Why did Toby call for his daddy at the end of the story?

When Toby woke up, he felt **dizzy** and weak. And oh, how his head hurt!

From far away he heard someone say, "He's coming to."

He opened his eyes. Why was he in bed? Who was that man in white looking down at him?

Toby rolled his eyes around. There were

Mother and Daddy on the other side of the bed. And then he saw a nurse coming in the door.

Was he in the hospital? What for?

He put his hand to his head and felt a thick **bandage**.

"Where am I?" he asked in a sleepy voice.

"You are in the **Emergency** Room," said Mother.

"Why? What happened?"

"I guess we really don't know," Daddy answered. "Mother heard a big bump on the front porch. She ran out and there you were lying on your back with **blood** running from your head. Do you remember what you were doing?"

Toby closed his eyes and tried to think. Oh, yes. He remembered. He had been counting cracks on the walk. He had made a running jump up onto the porch mat. That's the last he remembered anything.

Toby thought counting cracks in the sidewalk would sound silly to the doctor, so he said, "I tried to jump up on the porch without going up the steps."

"Now I think I know what happened," said Mother. "The porch mat slid when you landed on it. You fell back and hit your head on the edge of the porch."

"An ugly cut," said the doctor. "You are a lucky young man. You so easily could have had a **concussion**. But I don't think you do."

Toby didn't know what a concussion was. It sounded bad, and, well, sort of interesting.

"It wasn't luck," said Daddy with a smile at the doctor. "It was God taking care of a boy trying to do something sort of silly."

Then Daddy smiled at Toby too, so he knew Daddy wasn't cross.

"Well, take him home and keep him in bed for a few days. He should not be running around. Watch that cut so it doesn't start bleeding again. Put on a clean bandage every day and call me if you have any questions.

"And you, young man," he said with a friendly pat on Toby's leg. "Next time, walk up the steps." And the doctor went out.

———————✦———————

At home, Toby was glad to lie down. He felt a little dizzy. And he could feel every beat of his heart under that thick bandage on the back of his head.

He dozed off to sleep, but woke up when Mother came in. She had an orange popsicle in a dish.

"Daddy went down to the store and got a whole box. He said to let you have one any time you want one. He knows how you like popsicles."

"Oh, well, uh, thanks, Mother," said Toby.

Mother went out. Toby picked up the popsicle. Slowly he took off the wrapper. Slowly he folded it and put it on the chair beside his bed. He began to suck on the popsicle.

When Mother brought in supper on a tray, he wasn't a bit hungry. "I'm sorry," he said.

"That's all right, Toby," Mother said. "You have had quite a time. You gave us a real scare. But God was good to us and you will feel better tomorrow. Why don't you just go on to sleep?"

"All right." Toby turned on his side and shut his eyes. But he did not go to sleep for a long time. His head hurt and he could not stop thinking about that orange popsicle he had gotten after school.

Toby did feel better the next day. He got tired of staying in bed. And he could not stop thinking about the quarter he had not put in the basket at Sunday school.

After supper he was lying there thinking. Suddenly the door **burst** open.

"Surprise! Surprise!" shouted half a dozen voices. Into his room pushed his Sunday school class and his teacher.

"We came to give you a get-well party," said one.

"Can we see your cut?"

"Say, fellows, look at his big bandage!"

"Hey, they cut off his hair back there!"

"Does it hurt real bad?"

Toby sat there grinning happily and let them look at his bandage. Daddy brought in chairs. Mother brought in cake and ice cream.

His friends sat around his bed, eating and talking and laughing. They told about what

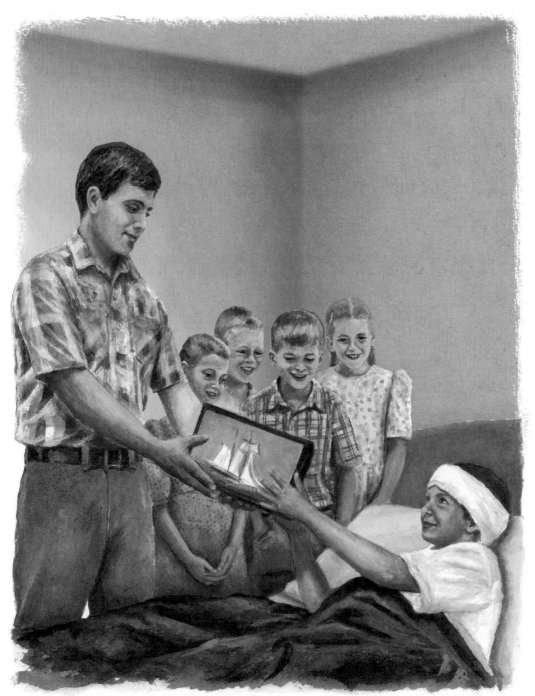

had happened at school that day.

After Mother had taken away the plates, the teacher went out. He came in with a package for Toby. "It is something for you to do while you must stay in bed," he said.

Toby squealed with delight when he opened it. It was a **model** ship for him to put together.

"Well, thank you. Thanks a lot, all of you," said Toby.

"We got it with the Sunday school class money," said one of the boys.

"Oh," said Toby. "Well, thanks again."

Then they all took one last look at Toby's bandage and said good-bye.

Toby said good-bye too.

After they had gone, he began to think so hard his head began to hurt again.

"They got me this model ship with the

class collection money! I guess they do other nice things like this with the class money. And here I am, not wanting to put any money in the basket. I'm just thinking about myself, and getting a prize for myself with popsicle wrappers.

"Now I have this ship that they bought with the money the other children gave."

Toby was feeling pretty bad by now. And he couldn't stop thinking about the orange popsicle.

"Daddy gave that quarter for me to put in the Sunday school basket. So it wasn't mine, after all. That means I stole that popsicle yesterday."

Toby sat there in bed feeling worse and worse.

At last he called, "Daddy, would you come here a minute?"

– Milo Kauffman

Toby spent his money for popsicles. The child in this poem had his mind on something other than popsicles.

The Animal Store

If I had a hundred dollars to spend,
　　Or maybe a little more,
I'd hurry as fast as my legs would go
　　Straight to the animal store.

I wouldn't say, "How much for this or that?"
　　"What kind of dog is he?"
I'd buy as many as rolled an eye
　　Or wagged a tail at me!

I'd take the hound with the drooping ears
　　That sits by himself alone;
Cockers and cairns and wobbly pups
　　For to be my very own.

I might buy a parrot all red and green,
And the monkey I saw before,
If I had a hundred dollars to spend,
Or maybe a little more.

– Rachel Field

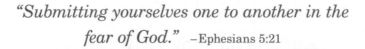
Secret of a Giver-Inner

Why did Ella Mae look so glum when
she got her own way all the time?

"I wonder why Ella Mae looks so glum," said Grandmother Lutz to herself. "She and Jill have been playing out there all morning. I have not seen her smile one time. But Jill seems to be having a good time."

Grandmother was sitting on her back porch. She watched her two granddaughters playing in her backyard.

Ella Mae lived in a white house on one side

of Grandmother's. Jill lived in a yellow house on the other side.

In the summertime the two girls **frequently** played in Grandmother's back-yard. There the huge maple trees made cool shade. On rainy days the girls played in the old shed that they had fixed up for a playhouse.

This morning as Grandmother sat watching the cousins going in and out of the playhouse, she said to herself, "I am going to find out what is wrong. Why does Jill look happy and Ella Mae look so glum? I hope they have not been **quarreling**."

Just then Ella Mae came out of the playhouse alone. She walked to the gate that led into her own yard.

Then Grandmother called, "Ella Mae, would you come here a minute?"

Ella Mae came and stood at the back steps.

"You don't look very happy," said Grandmother. "I hope you and Jill have not been quarreling. I can't have quarreling in my backyard, you know."

Ella Mae's eyes opened wide. "Oh, no, Grandmother. We weren't quarreling. Jill and I hardly ever quarrel. I am going home because it's lunchtime, not because we were fussing."

"Where is Jill?"

"She is still in the playhouse. She wasn't done with the dishes," said Ella Mae.

"The dishes?"

"Yes. I was the mother and she was the **hired** girl. Doing dishes is the hired girl's job. I said she should finish them before she went to lunch."

"I see," said Grandmother. "Do you play that game frequently?"

"Oh, yes. We play Mother and Hired Girl lots of times. We like to play that."

"Is Jill always the hired girl?"

"Sure. I'm the oldest, so I get to be the mother."

"You aren't very much older than Jill. Anyway, when you are pretending, it does not matter how old you really are.

"I remember when my sister and I played house. She was two years older than I, but lots of times she was the baby, because I liked to be the mother too, sometimes.

"Doesn't Jill get tired of being hired girl?"

"She used to. That's when we fussed sometimes. I guess that's why you think I looked unhappy. I do get tired of Jill trying to be what I want to be," said Ella Mae.

"Does she do that often?" asked Grandmother.

"No. Hardly ever anymore. But she used to do it when we played Nurse and Sick Old Lady too. She tried to make me let her be the nurse."

"Since you are the oldest, shouldn't you be the sick old lady, and let her be the nurse?"

"Oh, no," said Ella Mae. "The nurse kit belongs to me, so I get to be the nurse."

"I see. And what does Jill say when you make her be the hired girl and the sick old lady every time?"

"Well, she used to beg and beg and nearly cry. But now she just says, 'All right.' So things go fine and we have a good time."

"Why aren't you happy then, if you get to be what you want to be every time?" asked Grandmother.

"I *am* happy," said Ella Mae, smiling at Grandmother. "I guess I just get tired of Jill wanting to be what I want to be."

Then Ella Mae left and went through the gate into her own yard.

Soon Jill came from the playhouse. She looked toward the porch, then waved and called, "Hi, Grandmother. Thanks for letting us play in your yard again."

"Would you come here a minute?" called Grandmother.

Jill ran up the steps and dropped into the other rocking chair. She pretended to wipe **sweat** from her forehead. "Whew! That Mrs. Ella Mae really makes me work! And the babies were so fussy, and cried all the time. And there was such a stack of dishes! Am I ever glad it is lunchtime." Jill laughed and wiped away some more sweat.

"What were you playing?" asked Grandmother.

"Oh, we were playing Mother and Hired

Girl. That's fun."

"How do you play that?"

"Well, Ella Mae is the mother. She takes care of the three babies. She dresses them and

takes them for walks and puts them in for their naps and things like that.

"I'm the hired girl. I clean the house and make the meals, and do the dishes, and wash the clothes."

"Are you always the hired girl when you play that?"

"Yes. Ella Mae is older than I, you know."

"Don't you think it would be fun to be the mother sometimes?"

The smile left Jill's face. "Yes, I do," she said. "And I'd like to be nurse when we play Nurse and Sick Old Lady. But I can't be that because the nurse kit belongs to Ella Mae."

"Don't you ever ask her to take turns being mother and nurse?"

"I used to, but I don't anymore. When Ella Mae doesn't want to do something, she just won't do it. That's all! So I have to give in.

"You see, when both of us want to do the same thing, one of us must be the giver-inner or we won't get to play anything."

Then the smile came back on Jill's face. "You know, Grandmother, Ella Mae and I used to quarrel a lot. But since I learned to be the giver-inner, we don't quarrel much at all. And we have a lot of fun."

Jill hopped off the rocker. "I must go for lunch now." Then she laughed. "Maybe this afternoon you will come out to the playhouse and be our sick old lady. That is what we are going to play this afternoon."

Grandmother laughed too. "No, thank you, Jill. I'd rather be a *well* old lady sitting here in my rocking chair. I am glad you have learned the secret of having a good time when you play with others. No wonder you have a smile on your face all the time. And I'm going to pass on that secret to a certain cousin of yours the first chance I get."

– Ruth K. Hobbs

Miracle Oil

How do we know this was a miracle?

1. Now there cried a certain woman of the wives of the sons of the prophets unto Elisha, saying, Thy servant my husband is dead; and thou knowest that thy servant did fear the Lord: and the **creditor** is come to take unto him my two sons to be **bondmen.**

2. And Elisha said unto her, What shall I do for thee? tell me, what hast thou in the house? And she said, Thine **handmaid** hath not any thing in the house, save a pot of oil.

3. Then he said, Go, borrow thee **vessels** abroad of all thy neighbours, even empty vessels; borrow not a few.

4. And when thou art come in, thou shalt shut the door upon thee and upon thy sons, and shalt pour out into all those vessels, and thou shalt set aside that which is full.

5. So she went from him, and shut the door upon her and upon her sons, who brought the vessels to her; and she poured out.

6. And it came to pass, when the vessels were full, that she said unto her son, Bring me yet a vessel. And he said unto her, There is not a vessel more. And the oil stayed.

7. Then she came and told the man of God. And he said, Go, sell the oil, and pay thy debt, and live thou and thy children of the rest.

– 2 Kings 4:1-7

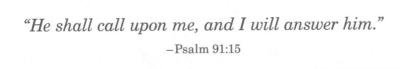

"He shall call upon me, and I will answer him."
—Psalm 91:15

A God Who Answers

A True Story

*How many of the children knew
the ship was on the way?*

"Is this all we get? I am still hungry," said
Figa. She looked down the long table. She
looked around the big dining room at all the
other tables. There was no more food on those
tables than on her own.

Figa lived in far-off **Egypt**. Egypt is the
land where Baby Moses was born. She was

an **orphan**. Her father and mother had been killed in the war. Now she lived in an **orphanage** with 450 other orphan girls. Their fathers and mothers had been killed in the war too. The orphan boys lived nearby in another building.

Mother **Trasher** was the head of the orphanage. She and her helpers loved God. They loved the orphans. They tried to make sure that all the girls had food and clothes. The girls went to school every day. They learned to love God.

But now Mother Trasher had no more money to buy food and clothes. The girls' dresses were **ragged**. At every meal the girls were given only a little bit to eat.

Mother Trasher hoped to make their food last until more money came. But no money came. Day after day there was less and less to eat. Now everyone was hungry.

At last, on a Monday afternoon, Mother Trasher sent a note to every helper in the orphanage. The note asked each helper to have a special prayer meeting. Everyone should ask God to send food and clothes.

The note said, "After supper the girls may pray as long and late as they wish. We have nothing. Our needs are great, but our God is greater. The Bible says, 'Ask, and it shall be given.' We will ask and He will answer."

After supper, Figa and all the other little ragged orphan girls gathered to pray.

Some prayed quietly. Some prayed out loud. Some prayed with tears running down their faces because they were so hungry.

Figa prayed, "Dear

Lord, You have said that when our mothers and fathers forsake us, then You will take us up. Please send us money so we can buy food and clothes."

The girls prayed a long time. As they fell asleep one by one, Mother Trasher carried them off to bed. A few kept praying until two o'clock in the morning.

On Tuesday, no one thought of school. They wanted to keep on praying. But no money came on Tuesday.

On Wednesday, Mother Trasher got a call to come to the big city. There she met a man from America.

He said, "Mother Trasher, a big ship was sent from America. It was full of food and clothes for poor people in the war country. When the ship got there, it could not stop at that country. So it came down to your **seaport** in Egypt.

"Now they do not know what to do with all the food and clothes. The ship is waiting at the seaport right now. Could you use those things at your orphanage?"

Could she!

On Thursday, the American man went to the seaport. He had the things taken off the ship and put on trucks.

On Friday, Figa and all the other children heard the sound of many trucks. They ran out to see.

Down the road came a long line of trucks. They stopped at Mother Trasher's house. Men began to take off the boxes and bags and **barrels.** They set them beside the road.

Mother Trasher and the other helpers came. They began to look in the boxes and barrels. Figa and the other children were wild with joy as they saw what had come.

There were thousands of dresses of all sizes for girls and women. There were thousands of shirts and pants of all sizes for boys and men. There were sweaters, blankets, towels, washcloths, and baby clothes.

There were hundreds of barrels of powdered milk, bags of rice, beans, and flour. There were thousands of cans of fruit and vegetables.

That Sunday there was a special thanksgiving service at the church. All the children wore new clothes. No one was hungry. No one was ragged.

Figa and the 450 girls who had prayed could not stop talking about their wonderful God who answers prayer.

– Basil Miller

In that dark night while the orphans prayed, God's love was bringing the shipload of food and clothes closer and closer. The girls did not know it, but it was a good night.

Good Night

Good night! Good night!
Far flies the light;
But still God's love
Shall flame above,
Making all bright.
Good night! Good night!

– Victor Hugo

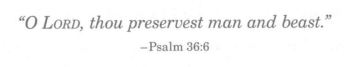

> *"O Lᴏʀᴅ, thou preservest man and beast."*
> —Psalm 36:6

The Saving of Spotsy

A True Story

*Could the keeper have saved Spotsy
in any other way?*

Spotsy was the tiny **fawn** of a Chinese water deer who lived in a New York zoo.

For a few days after he was born, no one but his mother knew it. Chinese water deer are very small. A big one is not nearly as large as a shepherd dog. And the fawns are only about ten inches tall.

Spotsy was so tiny his mother hid him in a clump of dry grass in the zoo field.

He lay very still. His spotted coat looked just like the grass clump. No one knew he was there except his mother.

The keeper of the Chinese water deer did not know Spotsy had been born. He did not see him in the grass.

For a few days Spotsy lay just where his mother hid him. She was never very far away. Now and then she would come to feed him and lick his spotted coat.

As he grew older, Spotsy did not like to obey his mother. He did not like to lie in the grass clump all the time.

His little legs were strong now. He began to get up and walk around.

After his mother fed him, she would push him down into the grass clump. "Obey me, Spotsy. Lie still now," she seemed to say.

Then she would go away to eat grass with the other Chinese water deer.

At last Spotsy did not want to obey his mother at all. His mother did not stay in a grass clump. Why should he? All the deer except him were out walking around in the grass.

One day he lay still until his mother was gone. Then he got up on his strong little legs. He began to walk away.

But he did not walk to his mother. He walked the other way.

Soon he came to a wire fence. The holes between the wires were too small for the grown-up deer to go through. But they were not too small for Spotsy.

He put his head and one leg through. Then he put the other front leg and his little spotted body through.

Three legs, four legs, through the wire

fence, and Spotsy was on the other side in a **strange** field.

Deer lived in this field too. But they were not Chinese water deer. They were big strong deer. They had sharp hoofs and sharp **antlers**. They were **dangerous**.

If these big deer saw a strange animal in their field, they would **attack** it. They would try to kill it with their sharp hoofs and antlers.

But Spotsy did not know these strange deer were dangerous. He did not know they would attack him if they saw him. They looked just like other deer to him.

He saw them in the middle of the field and began to walk through the tall grass toward them.

The grass was a few inches taller than Spotsy, so the dangerous deer did not see him coming.

Soon Spotsy's mother went to the grass clump to feed him. Spotsy was not there. She ran around the field looking for him. She called him, but he did not answer.

How could he answer when he was far away in the other field?

Then she saw him. She ran to the wire fence. But she could not get over it or through it. All she could do was watch him walking closer and closer to the dangerous deer.

Just then the keeper of the Chinese water deer came along. He had a bucket of grain for them.

All the other water deer ran to him for the grain. All except Spotsy's mother. She did not go to meet him as she always did before.

The keeper looked for her. He saw her running back and forth along the fence. That was strange. What was she looking at across the fence?

The keeper looked too. Then he saw Spotsy. In just a minute the little fawn would walk out of the tall grass. The dangerous deer would be sure to see and attack him then. None of them had spied him yet. They all were eating grass.

The keeper thought fast. He ran to the feedhouse in the other field. The dangerous deer always went there to get their grain. He banged the bucket on the side of the feedhouse. He wanted to draw the big deer away from Spotsy.

The dangerous deer looked up. They saw the keeper at the feedhouse with a bucket. They began to run toward the feedhouse for grain to eat.

As soon as they were all in the feedhouse, the keeper shut the door. He penned them all inside.

Now it was safe for him to go out and get
Spotsy.

He did not want to frighten the little fawn.
He walked toward him very slowly. Then he knelt
and held out his hand. Spotsy came up to sniff it.

The keeper put his hand around Spotsy to
draw him closer. Then he picked up the little

fawn. He took him back to the field where his mother was waiting.

The keeper let Spotsy's mother sniff her baby to know he was safe. But before he let Spotsy run in the field, he got a long, strong roll of chicken wire. He put it all along the bottom of the fence between Spotsy's field and the field where the dangerous deer were.

Now Spotsy had to obey his mother and stay in the field where he would be safe.

And you may be sure the keeper kept a sharp eye on the little spotted fawn.

– William Bridges

"I will keep the commandments of my God."

—Psalm 119:115

The Missing Crayons

A True Story

Some fathers in this story did something a
Christian father would not do. What was it?

Lazaro was a Toba Indian boy. He lived in
a house made of posts, mud, and grass.

Every morning he went to school. Every
Sunday he went to the mission church. Not
many of his school friends went to Sunday
school, but Lazaro loved to learn about Jesus.

One day on the way to school he caught

up with his two best friends. Their names were **Barbosa** and **Castillo**. They were talking to each other.

Barbosa was saying, "My father has no money to buy crayons for me."

"Neither does mine," said Castillo. "But I know what we can do. There are lots of boxes of crayons in the art cupboard at school. We could take a box. The teacher will not miss it. I do not think she knows how many boxes there are."

"Oh, but I don't want to get **caught** with crayons in my desk or in my pocket," said Barbosa. "What if the teacher would look for them and find them on me? It makes me **nervous** just to think about it."

Then Castillo said, "All we have to do is hide them till the end of school. We will be safe if we can just get them away from school, somehow."

"Yes, I guess that is right. We must think of a good way," said Barbosa. "Today we could get a box for me. Tomorrow we could get one for you. Or maybe we had better wait until next week. We should wait till the teacher forgets about the first box."

Many of the Toba Indians say it is all right to take other people's things if no one finds out who took them. They feel smart if they can steal something without being caught.

But Lazaro had been to Sunday school. He knew Jesus would not want him to steal.

Barbosa asked, "Will you help hide the crayons for us till the end of school?"

"No, I can't," said Lazaro. "Taking other people's things is stealing. Jesus said we should not steal."

"My father does not say it is wrong," said Barbosa. "He will be pleased with me if I am able to bring a box of crayons home without getting caught.

"But that is all right, Lazaro. Castillo is going to help. We will find a way without you."

And sure enough, they did. That day at the end of the coloring time, the teacher said, "There are a lot of crayons missing. I have the box, but not the crayons. Will all of you look for them?"

The teacher did not seem to see that Barbosa and Castillo were very nervous. She did not seem to see that most of the children were nervous too.

Everyone looked in his desk. Everyone shook his head. Then they all went out for recess.

After recess, the teacher again talked about the missing crayons. She said, "If anyone is hiding the crayons, will you please take them to the cupboard. We do not want to lose them. They belong to everyone."

No one said anything. Most of the children did not look at the teacher. No one began to look for the crayons again.

Then Lazaro guessed what Barbosa and Castillo had done.

They did not want the teacher to find any crayons in their pockets. A whole box was too hard to hide. So they had given each of the other children a crayon or two. They had asked the children to hide them. Then on the way home from school all the children were to give them to Barbosa. That way he would get a box of crayons for himself to have at home. That was why all the children acted so **guilty**.

The teacher looked at the children. Now she saw that none of them were looking at her. Some were looking at their desks. Some were looking at the floor. Some were looking out the window.

That is, all but Lazaro. He was looking right at her.

She said to him, "Lazaro, what do you think we should do about these missing crayons?"

Lazaro did not know what to do. He could not say he knew nothing about the crayons. He did not want to tell on his best friends. Neither did he want to help them get by with stealing. Jesus would not want him to help them do that.

Slowly he stood up beside his desk. He said, "At the mission Sunday school I learned that Jesus loves us all. He wants us all to do what is right so we will be happy. Jesus said that stealing is wrong. Stealing does not make you happy.

"Now any of you who have crayons may

bring them here to me."

No one moved for a minute. Then a little girl put her hand into her pocket. Out came a red crayon. She brought it and gave it to

Lazaro. She smiled as she went back to her desk.

One by one the other children pulled crayons from the places where they had hidden them. Soon Lazaro had almost the whole box on his desk.

He counted them. Four were still missing.

Now the children were happy again. They could look at the teacher. They could smile at her. Most of them had not wanted to hide crayons for the two boys who had stolen them. They were glad to be rid of them.

Lazaro still stood at his desk. He looked at Barbosa and at Castillo. All the boys and girls looked at Barbosa and Castillo.

Barbosa and Castillo did not look at anyone. They looked at the floor.

Suddenly Castillo got up and ran out the door. Barbosa ran out after him.

They went to the flower bed. They began digging with their hands. Soon they came back. Each had two crayons. They gave them to Lazaro.

Lazaro put the four crayons into the box. He gave the box to the teacher.

"Thank you, Lazaro," she said.

That day on the way home from school the Indian children began to sing "Jesus Loves Me."

Lazaro sang the loudest of all because Barbosa walked on one side of him. Castillo walked on the other side. Both of them were singing with him.

– Mary Ann Litwiller

Glossary

abode (ə•bōd) a place to live, *248*

African (ăf•rĭ•kən) something or someone from Africa, *168*

agreed (ə•grēd) thought or said the same as someone else did, *86*

Alps (ălps) a mountain range in Europe, *137*

amuse (ə•myüz) to help pass the time happily, *55*

antlers (ănt•lərz) the horns on a deer's head, *300*

approaching (ə•prōch•ĭng) coming nearer, *71*

apron (ā•prən) something worn over clothes to keep them clean, *235*

ashamed (ə•shāmd) feeling bad about doing something wrong, *221*

attack (ə•tăk) to start a fight, *300*

attempt (ə•tĕmpt) a try, *260*

attention (ə•tĕn•shən) listening to or looking at, *184*

bandage (băn•dĭj) a strip of cloth used to wrap a hurt place, *266*

Barbosa (bär•bō•sə) a boy's name, *306*

barefooted (bĕr•fút•əd) without shoes and socks, *1*

barrels (bĕr•əlz) large round containers, *293*

basement (bās•mənt) the lowest floor of a building, below or partly below the ground, *243*

beggar (bĕg•ər) someone who lives by asking others for money, clothes, and food, *79*

beneath (bē•nēth) below; under something, *234*

blood (bləd) the red liquid in your body, *266*

Brainerd (brā•nərd) a family's last name, *71*

burst (bərst) to break open suddenly with force, *270*

business (bĭz•nəs) something that a person should be interested in or busy with, *78*

cackled (kăk•əld) made the sound that a hen makes, *181*

camouflage (kăm•ə•flŏzh) color or shape that helps hide something, *48*

Castillo (kŏs•tē•yō) a boy's name, *306*

caught (kȯt) found out by someone, *306*

centavos (sĕn•tŏ•vōz) pieces of money from Mexico that are worth a small amount, *65*

certainly (sərt•ən•lē) without any doubt; surely, *2*

chattering (chăt•ər•ĭng) making sharp, quick sounds that sound like talking, *251*

Chinese checkers (chī•nēz chĕk•ərz) a game with a board and marbles, *54*

cliff dwellers (klĭf dwĕl•ərz) Indians who lived in or on cliffs, either in caves or in houses that they built, *18*

collection (kə•lĕk•shən) a group of things gathered together, *261*

Columbus (kə•ləm•bəs) the name of the sailor who found America, *201*

concussion (kən•kəsh•ən) an injury to the brain that comes from hitting the head very hard, *267*

confused (kən•fyüzd) feeling mixed up or not sure, *244*

cottage (kŏt•ĭj) a small house, *250*

counter (kount•ər) a high, long surface on which food is made, served, or eaten, *208*

crayfish (krā•físh) a small water creature, *31*

Creator (krē•āt•ər) God who created everything, *74*

creatures (krē•chərz) living things God created, *28*

crutches (krəch•əz) wooden or metal supports that help a person walk, *55*

dangerous (dān•jər•əs) likely to cause harm; not safe, *300*

dashed (dăsht) ran quickly, *29*

decide (dē•sīd) to make up your mind, *113*

despise (dĭ•spīz) to dislike very much; to hate, *111*

determined (dē•tər•mənd) to have your mind made up, *78*

disciples (dĭ•sī•pəlz) followers of a teacher, *248*

dizzy (dĭz•ē) unsteady; having the feeling of spinning, *265*

dodge (dŏj) to move quickly to get out of the way, *149*

dozen (dəz•ən) twelve, *235*

Egypt (ē•jĭpt) the name of a country, *289*

emergency (ē•mər•jən•sē) a serious happening that needs help right away, *266*

enemies (ĕn•ə•mēz) something that tries to hurt or kill another, *43*

enemy (ĕn•ə•mē) a person who dislikes another person, *194*

escape (ĕ•skāp) to get away, usually from danger, *48*

evil (ē•vəl) something that is very bad or wicked, *72*

except (ĕk•**sĕpt**) but; other than, *148*

explain (ĕk•**splān**) to make easy to understand, *247*

extra (**ĕks**•trə) more than enough, *236*

fawn (fȯn) a baby deer, *297*

Figa (**fē**•gə) a girl's name, *289*

finished (**fĭn**•ĭsht) ended; done, *64*

fractions (**frăk**•shənz) parts of a whole, such as ¼ and ½, *124*

frequently (**frē**•kwənt•lē) happening often, *277*

gathered (**găth**•ərd) came together in a group, *248*

glanced (glănst) gave a quick look at, *55*

groundhogs (**ground**•hȯgz) animals with fat bodies and brown fur; also called woodchucks, *31*

guilty (**gĭl**•tē) the feeling of having done wrong, *309*

habit (**hăb**•ĭt) something a person does for so long without thinking that it becomes hard to stop, *1*

hermit crab (**hər**•mĭt krăb) a creature that lives near water and uses an empty shell for a house, *34*

hinges (**hĭnj**•əz) metal pieces that let a door swing open and shut, *66*

hired (hīrd) paid to do a job, *278*

hobo (**hō**•bō) a person who wanders about from place to place, *87*

holy (**hō**•lē) set apart to God, *204*

Holy Spirit (**hō**•lē **spĭr**•ĭt) the Spirit of God, *70*

homemade (**hōm**•mād) made at home, *192*

hornets (hȯr•nəts) insects that sting, *33*

huge (hyüj) very large, *251*

humble (həm•bəl) not acting proud, *248*

ignore (ĭg•nȯr) to pay no attention to, *78*

imagine (ĭ•măj•ĭn) to get a picture or idea in your mind, *55*

inspector (ĭn•spĕk•tər) a person who looks at something to see if it is done correctly, *83*

instant (ĭn•stənt) almost right away, *138*

instructions (ĭn•strək•shənz) directions; orders, *102*

invalid (ĭn•və•ləd) a person who is sick or unable to move in a normal way, especially for a long time, *87*

invitation (ĭn•və•tā•shən) a request to come to something, *209*

Irmgard (ərm•gärd) a girl's name, *135*

jingle (jĭng•gəl) to make a ringing, tinkling sound, like metal striking together, *66*

Josie (jō•sē) a girl's name, *193*

jungle (jəng•gəl) a thick growth of trees and plants that covers a large area, *167*

kerosene (kər•ə•sēn) a thin, light-colored oil, *77*

layer (lā•ər) a hen that lays eggs, *180*

Lazaro (lə•zŏ•dō) a boy's name, *305*

Lusa (lü•sə) a girl's name, *166*

Manning (măn•ĭng) a family's last name, *166*

Mario (mŏ•dĭ•ō) a boy's name, *250*

marketplace (mär•kət•plās) a place to buy and sell things, *250*

marvelous (mär•və•ləs) wonderful, *30*

medicine (mĕ•də•sən) something used to cure a sickness, *166*

memorized (mĕm•ə•rīzd) learned every word by heart, *79*

merchants (mər•chənts) people who buy and sell things, *223*

message (mĕs•ĭj) facts or news sent from one person to another, *135*

Mexico (mĕk•sĭ•kō) a country south of the United States, *64*

midst (mĭdst) middle or part of, *248*

millions (mĭl•yənz) a very large number, *202*

mistake (mĭ•stāk) an answer or idea that is wrong, *209*

model (mŏd•əl) a small copy of something, *272*

mortar (mȯrt•ər) a mixture that is used to hold bricks or stones together, *18*

muskrats (məsk•răts) small brown furry animals that live in or near water, *31*

mystery (mĭs•tər•ē) something that cannot be explained, *221*

necessary (nĕs•ə•sĕr•ē) needed, *102*

nervous (nər•vəs) feeling uneasy; being anxious, *306*

nuisance (nü•səns) something that bothers, *2*

office (ȯf•əs) a room where a person works at a desk, *149*

opportunity (ŏp•ər•tü•nə•tē) a chance to do something, *211*

ordinary (ȯr•də•nĕr•ē) normal; usual, *103*

orphan (ȯr•fən) a child whose parents have both died, *290*

orphanage (ȯr•fən•ĭj) a home for orphans, *290*

oxcart (ŏks•kärt) a two-wheeled wagon pulled by an ox, *221*

Pablo (pŏ·blō) a boy's name, *64*

palace (păl·əs) the large home of a ruler, *220*

pasture (păs·chər) a field where animals eat grass, *89*

patient (pā·shənt) willing to wait without complaining, *125*

peacemakers (pēs·māk·ərz) people who stop arguments or fights, *195*

pegging (pĕg·ĭng) working steadily without stopping, *131*

plains (plānz) large stretches of flat land, *15*

plodded (plŏd·əd) walked along in a slow, steady way, *204*

popsicles (pŏp·sĭ·kəlz) colored and flavored water frozen on sticks, *257*

positive (pŏz·ə·tĭv) without doubt; sure, *69*

posted (pōst·əd) put up for all to see, *234*

poured (pȯrd) made something flow out, *129*

principal (prĭn·sə·pəl) the person who is in charge of a school, *148*

probably (prŏb·ə·blē) very likely, *194*

protect (prō·tĕkt) to keep safe, *22*

puzzled (pəz·əld) confused; not understanding, *104*

quarreling (kwȯr·lĭng) arguing or disagreeing, *277*

ragged (răg·əd) torn and worn out, *290*

rapped (răpt) knocked quickly and sharply, *82*

realized (rē·ə·līzd) understood fully, *103*

reward (rē·wȯrd) a prize given for a job well done, *87*

roaming (rōm·ĭng) going around from place to place, *28*

rude (rüd) treating others badly; not polite, *103*

Saddhu (sŏ•dü) a boy's name, *77*

salvation (săl•vā•shən) the saving of a soul from evil and death, *70*

sandstone (sănd•stōn) a kind of rock made from sand held together with lime, *18*

satisfy (săt•ĭs•fī) to meet the needs or wishes of, *112*

scolding (skōld•ĭng) talking in anger, *221*

scouts (skouts) people who are sent to find out things, *72*

scratching (skrăch•ĭng) scraping with claws or fingernails, *180*

seaport (sē•pȯrt) a town close to the sea where ships stop to load or unload, *292*

select (sə•lĕkt) to choose or pick, *112*

sense (sĕns) something you can understand, *125*

shelters (shĕl•tərz) roofs or walls that protect from the weather or enemies, *16*

slushy (sləsh•ē) partly melted, *261*

something (səm•thĭng) a thing that is not named or known for sure, *10*

sparrow (spĕr•ō) a small, brownish-gray bird, *182*

station (stā•shən) a place where a train stops to load and unload people, *203*

strange (strānj) not known before; unusual, *300*

strawberry (strȯ•bĕr•ē) a sweet red fruit with seeds on the outside, *198*

sucked (səkt) drew in liquid with the mouth, *258*

sweat (swĕt) water drops on your skin when you are hot, *281*

Swiss (swĭs) something or someone from Switzerland, *135*

Switzerland (swĭt•sər•lənd) the name of a country with high mountains, *135*

swollen (swō•lən) big and puffed up, *166*

tepee (tē•pē) a round house made of poles covered with animal skins, *16*

terrible (tĕr•ə•bəl) very bad, *167*

tinkle (tĭngk•əl) a light, ringing sound, *138*

trail (trāl) a path, *252*

Trasher (trăsh•ər) a family's last name, *290*

tribes (trībz) groups of people who lived under one leader or chief, *16*

usually (yü•zhü•ə•lē) used most often, *167*

Wembo (wĕm•bō) a boy's name, *166*

wickiup (wĭk•ē•əp) a round house made of poles covered with grass mats, *17*

wigwam (wĭg•wŏm) a round house made of poles covered with bark, grass mats, or animal skins, *17*

wilderness (wĭl•dər•nəs) a wild country; land where no one lives, *95*

witch doctor (wĭch dŏk•tər) a person who tries to cure sickness with evil power, *169*

worry (wər•ē) to feel fearful, *151*

wrappers (răp•ərz) pieces of paper used to wrap things, *258*

Acknowledgements

Artist: Shirley Myers and others

Cover design: David Miller

Editorial committee: Ben Bergen, Keith E. Crider, James Hershberger, Sadie Schrock

"A Chance for This and a Chance for That," adapted from "A Plan for Getting Even," by Marion Ullmark, *Beams of Light,* July, 1957. Mennonite Publishing House, Scottdale, PA. Used by permission.

"A God Who Answers," adapted from *Nineteen Missionary Stories from the Middle East* by Basil Miller. Copyright ©1950 by Zondervan Publishing House. Used by permission of Zondervan Publishing House.

"A Good Plan," Author Unknown.

"A Story in the Snow," by Pearl Riggs Crouch.

"All Kinds of Houses," by Ruth K. Hobbs. ©1999 Christian Light Publications, Inc. All rights reserved.

"Andy's Real Question," adapted from "Andy's Big Question," by Edna Beiler, from *Beams of Light.* Used by permission of *The Old Country News,* Millersburg, PA.

"Autumn," by Persis Gardiner.

"Baby Seeds," from *Very Young Verses.*

"Chanticleer," by John Farrar, from *Songs for Parents.*

"Cow with a Secret," adapted from "Irmgard's Cow," by Maud Lindsay, *The Child's World,* Second Reader.

"Enemy or Peacemaker?" adapted from "The Little Peacemaker," by Grace Cash, *Beams of Light,* August, 1956. Mennonite Publishing House, Scottdale, PA. Used by permission.

"Five Little Brothers," by Ella Wheeler Wilcox.

"Four Thousand for Dinner," from Mark 8, KJV.

"Golden Rule Corn," adapted from "How Many Ears in a Dozen," by Mary Hursh. ©1993 Mary Hursh. Used by permission.

"Good Night," by Victor Hugo.

"Happy Hearts," by Merna B. Shank. ©1998 Christian Light Publications, Inc., Harrisonburg, VA. All rights reserved.

"Here Comes the Principal," by Ruth K. Hobbs. ©1999 Christian Light Publications, Inc. All rights reserved.

"I Know, I Know, I Know," adapted from "Big Brown Box," by Eileen M. Hasse, *Beams of Light,* March, 1956. Mennonite Publishing House, Scottdale, PA. Used by permission.

"Linda Lou's Special Day," adapted from "Linda Lou's Special Day," by Ruth K. Hobbs, *Story Friends,* June, 1961. Mennonite Publishing House, Scottdale, PA. Used by permission.

"Lost and Found," from *Poems for our Boys and Girls.*

"Mario and the Monkeys," adapted from a South American folk tale.

"Message From the Sky," from Luke 2, KJV.

"Miracle Oil," from 2 Kings, KJV.

"Money in His Pocket," by Dorothy Ballard.

"Mrs. Cut-Cut's Close Call," adapted from "White Hen," by Leah Kauffman Lind, *Beams of Light,* July 29, 1956. Mennonite Publishing House, Scottdale, PA. Used by permission.

"My Dog," by Marchette Chute, from *Rhymes About Ourselves.*

"Overheard in an Orchard," by Elizabeth Cheney.

"Rock-A-By, Hush-A-By, Little Papoose," by Charles Myali.

"Secret of a Giver-Inner," by Ruth K. Hobbs. ©1999 Christian Light Publications, Inc. All rights reserved.

"Seen Through the Tent Door," adapted from *Beams of Light.*

"Snow Camel for Beth," by Ruth K. Hobbs. ©1999 Christian Light Publications, Inc. All right reserved.

"Sticking With It," adapted from "By Keeping At It," Author Unknown, *Beams of Light,* December, 1922. Mennonite Publishing House, Scottdale, PA. Used by permission.

"Taking Off," by Mary McB. Green, from *Very Young Verses.*

"Ten Little Duties," from *Poems for our Boys and Girls.*

"The Animal Store," by Rachel Field, from *Taxis and Toadstools.*

"The Boy Who Determined to Learn," adapted from "The Boy Who Wanted to Go to School," by Rhoda R. Eby, *Beams of Light,* May, 1921. Mennonite Publishing House, Scottdale, PA. Used by permission.

"The Fall of Jericho," from Joshua, KJV.

"The Flying Stars," from *Analytical Second Reader.*

"The Hairy Dog," by Herbert Asquith.

"The House of the Mouse," from *Another Here and Now Story Book* by Lucy Sprague Mitchell, copyright 1937 by E. P. Dutton, renewed ©1965 by Lucy Sprague Mitchell. Used by permission of Dutton Children's Books, a division of Penguin Young Readers Group, A member of Penguin Group (USA) Inc., 345 Hudson Street, New York, NY 10014. All rights reserved.

"The Iron That Floated," from 2 Kings, KJV.

"The Jolly Woodchuck," reprinted with the permission of Atheneum Books for Young Readers, an imprint of Simon & Schuster Children's Publishing Division from *Open the Door* by Marion Edey and Dorothy Grider (Charles Scribner's Sons, NY, 1949).

"The Lost Shoes," adapted from "Nellie's Lost Shoe," by Elva E. Leaman, *Beams of Light.*

"The Missing Crayons," adapted from "The Missing Crayons," by Mary Ann Litwiller, *Beams of Light,* January 1956. Mennonite Publishing House, Scottdale, PA. Used by permission.

"The Mystery Stone," adapted from "The Stone in the Road," *The Child's World,* Second Reader.

"The New Baby Calf," by Edith H. Newlin.

"The Red Children," adapted from "The Red Children," *Graded Classics,* Second Reader.

"The Saving of Spotsy," adapted from "The Saving of Spotsy" by William Bridges, *Zoo Babies.*

"The Snowman," by Francis Frost.

"The Stolen Popsicle," adapted from "The Popsicle," by Milo Kauffman, *Beams of Light,* November, 1956. Mennonite Publishing House, Scottdale, PA. Used by permission.

"The Woodpecker," from *Under the Tree* by Elizabeth Madox Roberts.

"To Save Their Lives," by Ruth K. Hobbs. ©1999 Christian Light Publications, Inc. All rights reserved.

"What Happened in the Night," adapted from "Boys and Girls," Author Unknown, *Beams of Light,* April 1921. Mennonite Publishing House, Scottdale, PA. Used by permission.

"Which Loved Her Best?" by Joy Allison (Mary A. Cragin).

"Whom Shall I Fear?" adapted from "Wembo's Trust," Esther Miller Payler, *Beams of Light,* March, 1955. Mennonite Publishing House, Scottdale, PA. Used by permission.

Attempt has been made to secure permission for the use of all copyrighted material. If further information is received, the publisher will be glad to properly credit the material in future printings.